Foundational Python for Data Science

The Pearson Addison-Wesley Data & Analytics Series

Visit **informit.com/awdataseries** for a complete list of available publications.

The **Pearson Addison-Wesley Data & Analytics Series** provides readers with practical knowledge for solving problems and answering questions with data. Titles in this series primarily focus on three areas:

1. **Infrastructure:** how to store, move, and manage data
2. **Algorithms:** how to mine intelligence or make predictions based on data
3. **Visualizations:** how to represent data and insights in a meaningful and compelling way

The series aims to tie all three of these areas together to help the reader build end-to-end systems for fighting spam; making recommendations; building personalization; detecting trends, patterns, or problems; and gaining insight from the data exhaust of systems and user interactions.

Make sure to connect with us!
informit.com/socialconnect

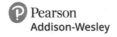
Pearson
Addison-Wesley

the trusted technology learning source

Foundational Python for Data Science

Kennedy R. Behrman

✦✦ Addison-Wesley

Boston • Columbus • New York • San Francisco • Amsterdam • Cape Town
Dubai • London • Madrid • Milan • Munich • Paris • Montreal • Toronto • Delhi • Mexico City
São Paulo • Sydney • Hong Kong • Seoul • Singapore • Taipei • Tokyo

For information about buying this title in bulk quantities, or for special sales opportunities (which may include electronic versions; custom cover designs; and content particular to your business, training goals, marketing focus, or branding interests), please contact our corporate sales department at corpsales@pearsoned.com or (800) 382-3419.

For government sales inquiries, please contact governmentsales@pearsoned.com.

For questions about sales outside the U.S., please contact intlcs@pearson.com.

Visit us on the Web: informit.com/aw.

Library of Congress Control Number: 2021940284

ISBN-13: 978-0-13-662435-6
ISBN-10: 0-13-662435-9

1 2021

Editor-in-Chief
Mark Taub

Acquisitions Editor
Malobika Chakraborty

Development Editor
Mark Renfrow

Managing Editor
Sandra Schroeder

Senior Project Editor
Lori Lyons

Copy Editor
Kitty Wilson

Production Manager
Aswini Kumar/ codeMantra

Indexer
Timothy Wright

Proofreader
Abigail Manheim

Compositor
codeMantra

❖

This book is dedicated to Tatiana, Itta, and Maple,
who is probably still under the bed.

❖

Contents at a Glance

Table of Contents

Preface

The Python language has been around for a long time and worn many hats. Its original implementation was started by Guido van Rossum in 1989 as a tool for system administration as an alternative to Bash scripts and C programs.[1] Since its public release in 1991, it has evolved for use in a myriad of industries. These include everything from web-development, film, government, science, and business.[2]

I was first introduced to Python working in the film industry, where we used it to automate data management across departments and locations. In the last decade, Python has become a dominant tool in Data Science.

This dominance evolved due to two developments: the Jupyter notebook, and powerful third-party libraries. In 2001 Fernando Perez began the IPython project, an interactive Python environment inspired by Maple and Mathematica notebooks.[3] By 2014, the notebook-specific part of the project was split off as the Jupyter project. These notebooks have excelled for scientific and statistical work environments. In parallel with this development, third-party libraries for scientific and statistical computing were developed for Python. With so many applications, the functionality available to a Python programmer has grown immensely. With specialized packages for everything from opening web sockets to processing natural language text, there is more available than a beginning developer needs.

This project was the brainchild of Noah Gift.[4] In his work as an educator, he found that students of Data Science did not have a resource to learn just the parts of Python they needed. There were many general Python books and books about Data Science, but not resources for learning just the Python needed to get started in Data Science. That is what we have attempted to provide here. This book will not teach the Python needed to set up a web page or perform system administration. It is also not intended to teach you Data Science, but rather the Python needed to learn Data Science.

I hope you will find this guide a good companion in your quest to grow your Data Science knowledge.

Example Code

Most of the code shown in examples in this book can be found on GitHub at: https://github.com/kbehrman/foundational-python-for-data-science.

---

1 https://docs.python.org/3/faq/general.html#why-was-python-created-in-the-first-place
2 https://www.python.org/success-stories/
3 http://blog.fperez.org/2012/01/ipython-notebook-historical.html
4 https://noahgift.com

Figure Credits

Figure	Credit Attribution
Cover	Boris Znaev/Shutterstock
Cover	Mark.G/Shutterstock
Figure 1-01	Screenshot of Colab Dialogue © 2021 Google
Figure 1-02	Screenshot of Renaming Notebook © 2021 Google
Figure 1-03	Screenshot of Google Drive © 2021 Google
Figure 1-04	Screenshot of Editing Text Cells © 2021 Google
Figure 1-05	Screenshot of Formatting Text © 2021 Google
Figure 1-06	Screenshot of Lists © 2021 Google
Figure 1-07	Screenshot of Headings © 2021 Google
Figure 1-08	Screenshot of Table of Contents © 2021 Google
Figure 1-09	Screenshot of Hiding Cells © 2021 Google
Figure 1-10	Screenshot of LaTeX Example © 2021 Google
Figure 1-11	Screenshot of A Files © 2021 Google
Figure 1-12	Screenshot of Upload Files © 2021 Google
Figure 1-13	Screenshot of Mount Google Drive © 2021 Google
Figure 1-14	Screenshot of Code Snippets © 2021 Google

Register Your Book

Register your copy of *Foundational Python for Data Science* on the InformIT site for convenient access to updates and/or corrections as they become available. To start the registration process, go to informit.com/register and log in or create an account. Enter the product ISBN **9780136624356** and click Submit. Look on the Registered Products tab for an Access Bonus Content link next to this product, and follow that link to access any available bonus materials. If you would like to be notified of exclusive offers on new editions and updates, please check the box to receive email from us.

Acknowledgments

The idea for this book first came from Noah Gift. It is he who really identified the need for a specialized introduction to Python targeted at students of Data Science. Thank you for that, Noah. And thank you to Colin Erdman who, acting as technical editor, brought an attention to detail that was much appreciated and needed. I also want to thank the Pearson team, including Malobika Chakraborty, who guided me through the whole process, Mark Renfrow, who came in and helped get the project done, and Laura Lewin, who helped get it going.

About the Author

Kennedy Behrman is a veteran software engineer. He began using Python to manage digital assets in the visual effects industry and has used it extensively since. He has authored various books and training programs around Python education. He currently works as a senior data engineer at Envestnet.

Part I

Learning Python in a Notebook Environment

Introduction to Notebooks

All animals are equal, but some animals are more equal than others.

George Orwell

In This Chapter

- Running Python statements
- Introduction to Jupyter notebooks
- Introduction to Google Colab hosted notebooks
- Text and code cells
- Uploading files to the Colab environment
- Using a system alias to run shell commands
- Magic functions

This chapter introduces Google Colab's Jupyter notebook environment, which is a great way for a beginner to get started in scientific Python development. This chapter begins by looking at traditional ways of running Python code.

Running Python Statements

Historically, Python was invoked either in an interactive Python shell or by supplying text files to the interpreter. If you have Python installed on your system, you can open the Python built-in interactive shell by typing `python` at the command line:

```
python
Python 3.9.1 (default, Mar  7 2021, 09:53:19)
[Clang 12.0.0 (clang-1200.0.32.29)] on darwin
Type "help", "copyright", "credits" or "license" for more information.
```

> **Note**
>
> For code in this book, we use **bold text** for user input (the code you would type), and non-bold text for any output that results.

You can then type Python statements and run them by pressing Enter:

```
print("Hello")
Hello
```

As shown here, you see the result of each statement displayed directly after the statement's line.

When Python commands are stored in a text file with the extension .py, you can run them on the command line by typing **python** followed by the filename. If you have a file named hello.py, for example, and it contains the statement `print("Hello")`, you can invoke this file on the command line as follows and see its output displayed on the next line:

```
python hello.py
Hello
```

For traditional Python software projects, the interactive shell was adequate as a place to figure out syntax or do simple experiments. The file-based code was where the real development took place and where software was written. These files could be distributed to whatever environment needed to run the code. For scientific computing, neither of these solutions was ideal. Scientists wanted to have interactive engagement with data while still being able to persist and share in a document-based format. Notebook-based development emerged to fill the gap.

Jupyter Notebooks

The IPython project is a more feature-rich version of the Python interactive shell. The Jupyter project sprang from the IPython project. Jupyter notebooks combine the interactive nature of the Python shell with the persistence of a document-based format. A notebook is an executable document that combines executable code with formatted text. A notebook is composed of *cells*, which contain code or text. When a code cell is executed, any output is displayed directly below the cell. Any state changes performed by a code cell are shared by any cells executed subsequently.

This means you can build up your code cell by cell, without having to rerun the whole document when you make a change. This is especially useful when you are exploring and experimenting with data.

Jupyter notebooks have been widely adopted for data science work. You can run these notebooks locally from your machine or from hosted services such as those provided by AWS, Kaggle, Databricks, or Google.

Google Colab

Colab (short for Colaboratory) is Google's hosted notebook service. Using Colab is a great way to get started with Python, as you don't need to install anything or deal with library dependencies or environment management. This book uses Colab notebooks for all of its examples. To use Colab, you must be signed in to a Google account and go to https://colab.research.google.com (see Figure 1.1). From here you can create new notebooks or open existing notebooks. The existing notebooks can include examples supplied by Google, notebooks you have previously created, or notebooks you have copied to your Google Drive.

Examples	Recent	Google Drive	GitHub	Upload

Filter notebooks

Title	First opened	Last opened	
CO Welcome To Colaboratory	3 days ago	0 minutes ago	
Untitled0.ipynb	0 minutes ago	0 minutes ago	
MyFirstNotebook.ipynb	3 days ago	3 days ago	
Chpt5-Other-Python-Data_Structures.ipynb	Dec 28, 2019	Dec 28, 2019	

NEW NOTEBOOK   CANCEL

Figure 1.1   The Initial Google Colab Dialog

When you choose to create a new notebook, it opens in a new browser tab. The first notebook you create has the default title Untitled0.ipynb. To change its name, double-click on the title and type a new name (see Figure 1.2).

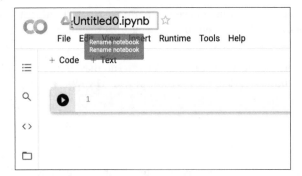

Figure 1.2   Renaming a Notebook in Google Colab

Colab automatically saves your notebooks to your Google Drive, which you can access by going to Drive.Google.com. The default location is a directory named Colab Notebooks (see Figure 1.3).

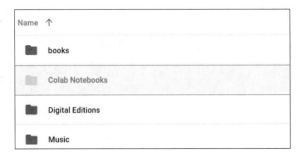

Figure 1.3   The Colab Notebooks Folder at Google Drive

Colab Text Cells

A new Google Colab notebook has a single code cell. A cell can be one of two types: text or code. You can add new cells by using the + Code and + Text buttons in the upper left of the notebook interface.

Text cells are formatted using a language called Markdown. (For more information on Markdown, see https://colab.research.google.com/notebooks/markdown_guide.ipynb.) To edit a cell, you double-click it, and the Markdown appears to the right, with a preview of its output to the left (see Figure 1.4).

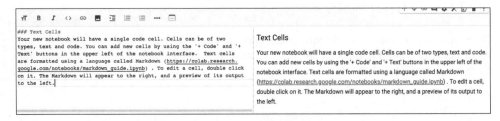

Figure 1.4   Editing Text Cells in a Google Colab Notebook

As shown in Figure 1.5, you can modify text in a notebook to be bold, italic, struck through, and monospaced.

Figure 1.5   Formatting Text in a Google Colab Notebook

As shown in Figure 1.6, you can create a numbered list by prefacing items with numbers, and you can create a bulleted list by prefacing items with stars.

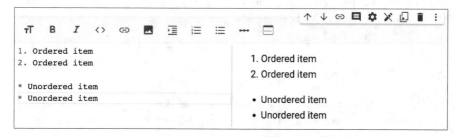

Figure 1.6   Creating Lists in a Google Colab Notebook

As shown in Figure 1.7, you can create headings by preceding text with hash signs. A single hash sign creates a top-level heading, two hashes creates a first level heading, and so forth.

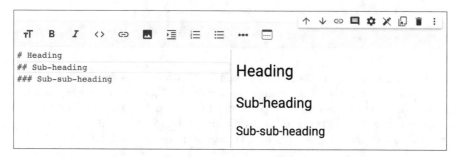

Figure 1.7   Creating Headings in a Google Colab Notebook

A heading that is at the top of a cell determines the cell's hierarchy in the document. You can view this hierarchy by opening the table of contents, which you do by clicking the Menu button at the top left of the notebook interface, as shown in Figure 1.8.

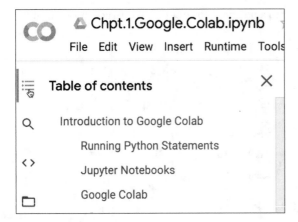

Figure 1.8   The Table of Contents in a Google Colab Notebook

You can use the table of contents to navigate the document by clicking on the displayed headings. A heading cell that has child cells has a triangle next to the heading text. You can click this triangle to hide or view the child cells (see Figure 1.9).

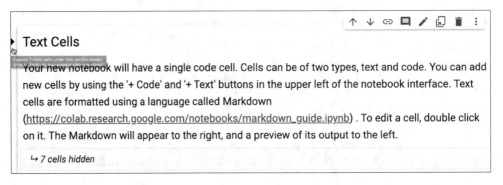

Figure 1.9   Hiding Cells in a Google Colab Notebook

LaTeX

The LaTeX language (see https://www.latex-project.org/about/), which is designed for preparing technical documents, excels at presenting mathematical text. LaTeX uses a code-based approach that is designed to allow you to concentrate on content rather than layout. You can insert LaTeX code into Colab notebook text cells by surrounding it with dollar signs. Figure 1.10 shows an example from the LaTeX documentation embedded in a Colab notebook text cell.

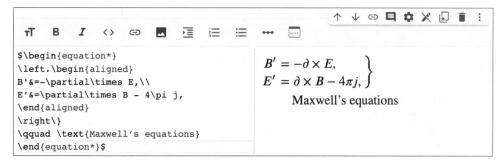

Figure 1.10   LaTeX Embedded in a Google Colab Notebook

Colab Code Cells

In Google Colab notebooks, you use code cells to write and execute Python code. To execute a Python statement, you type it into a code cell and either click the Play button at the left of the cell or press Shift+Enter. Pressing Shift+Enter takes you to the next cell or creates a new cell if there are none following. Any output from the code you execute is displayed below the cell, as in this example:

```
print("Hello")
hello
```

Subsequent chapters of this book use only code cells for Colab notebooks.

Colab Files

To see the files and folders available in Colab, click the Files button on the left of the interface (see Figure 1.11). By default, you have access to the sample_data folder supplied by Google.

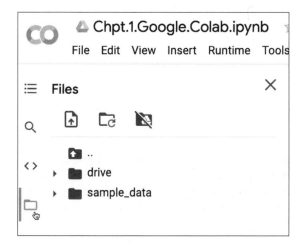

Figure 1.11   Viewing Files in Google Colab

You can also click the Upload button to upload files to the session (see Figure 1.12).

Figure 1.12   Uploading Files in Google Colab

Files that you upload are available only in the current session of your document. If you come back to the same document later, you need to upload them again. All files available in Colab have the path root /content/, so if you upload a file named heights.over.time.csv, its path is /content/heights.over.time.csv.

You can mount your Google Drive by clicking the Mount Drive button (see Figure 1.13). The contents of you drive have the root path /content/drive.

Figure 1.13   Mounting Your Google Drive

Managing Colab Documents

By default, notebooks are saved to your Google Drive. In the File menu you can see other options for saving notebooks. You can save them to GitHub, either as gists or as tracked files. You can also download them either in Jupyter notebook format (with the .ipynb extension) or as Python files (with the .py extension). You can also share notebooks by clicking the Share button in the upper right of the notebook interface.

Colab Code Snippets

The Code Snippets section of the left navigation section of Colab lets you search and select code snippets (see Figure 1.14). You can insert selected snippets by clicking the Insert button. Using code snippets is a great way to see examples of what can be done in Colab, including making interactive forms, downloading data, and using various visualization options.

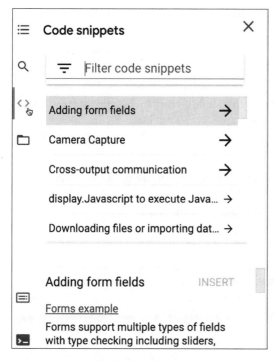

Figure 1.14   Using Code Snippets in Google Colab

Existing Collections

You can use Google Colab notebooks to explain and demonstrate techniques, concepts, and workflows. Data science work is shared in many collections of notebooks available around the web. Kaggle (see https://www.kaggle.com/code) has plenty of shared notebooks, as does the Google Seedbank (see https://research.google.com/seedbank/).

System Aliases

You can run a shell command from within a Colab notebook code cell by prepending the command with an exclamation point. For example, the following example prints the working directory:

```
!pwd
/content
```

You can capture any output from a shell command in a Python variable, as shown here, and use it in subsequent code:

```
var = !ls sample_data
print(var)
```

> **Note**
>
> Don't worry about variables yet. You will learn about them in Chapter 2, "Fundamentals of Python."

Magic Functions

Magic functions are functions that change the way a code cell is run. For example, you can time a Python statement by using the magic function `%timeit()` as shown here:

```
import time
%timeit(time.sleep(1))
```

As another example, you can have a cell run HTML code by using the magic function `%%html`:

```
%%html
<marquee style='width: 30%; color: blue;'><b>Whee!</b></marquee>
```

> **Note**
>
> You can find more information about magic functions in Cell Magics example notebooks that is part of the Jupyter documentation at https://nbviewer.jupyter.org/github/ipython/ipython/blob/1.x/examples/notebooks/Cell%20Magics.ipynb.

Summary

Jupyter notebooks are documents that combine formatted text with executable code. They have become a very popular format for scientific work, and many examples are available around the web. Google Colab offers hosted notebooks and includes many popular libraries used in data science. A notebook is made up of text cells, which are formatted in Markdown, and code cells, which can execute Python code. The following chapters present many examples of Colab notebooks.

Questions

1. What kind of notebooks are hosted in Google Colab?

2. What cell types are available in Google Colab?

3. How do you mount your Google Drive in Colab?

4. What language runs in Google Colab code cells?

Fundamentals of Python

All models are wrong, but some are useful.

George E.P. Box

In This Chapter

- Python built-in types
- Introduction to statements
- Expression statements
- Assert statements
- Assignment statements and variables
- Import statements
- Printing
- Basic math operations
- Dot notation

This chapter looks at some of the building blocks you can use to create a Python program. It introduces the basic built-in data types, such as integers and strings. It also introduces various simple statements you can use to direct your computer's actions. This chapter covers statements that assign values to variables and statements to ensure that code evaluates as expected. It also discusses how to import modules to extend the functionality available to you in your code. By the end of this chapter, you will have enough knowledge to write a program that performs simple math operations on stored values.

Basic Types in Python

Biologists find it useful to organize living things into a hierarchy from domain and kingdom down to genus and species. The lower down this hierarchy you go, the more alike the life-forms that share a group. A similar hierarchy exists in data science.

A *parser* is a program that takes your code as input and translates it into instructions to a computer. The Python parser breaks up your code into tokens, which have particular meaning defined for the Python language. It is useful to group these tokens based on shared behaviors and attributes, much as biologists do with beings in nature. These groups in Python are called *collections* and *types*. There are types that are built into the language itself, and there are types that are defined by developers outside the language core. At a high level, the Python documentation (see https://docs.python.org/3/library/stdtypes.html) defines the principal built-in types as numerics, sequences (see Chapter 3, "Sequences"), mappings (see Chapter 4, "Other Data Structures"), classes (see Chapter 14, "Object-Oriented Programming"), instances (see Chapter 14), and exceptions. At a low level, the most basic built-in types are as follows:

- **Numerics:** Booleans, integers, floating point numbers, and imaginary numbers
- **Sequences:** Strings and binary strings

At the simplest, integers (or ints) are represented in code as ordinary digits. Floating point numbers, referred to as floats, are represented as a group of digits including a dot separator. You can use the type function to see the type of an integer and a float:

```
type(13)
int
```

```
type(4.1)
float
```

If you want a number to be a float, you must ensure that it has a dot and a number to the right, even if that number is zero:

```
type(1.0)
float
```

Booleans are represented by the two constants, True and False, both of which evaluate to the type bool, which, behind the scenes, is a specialized form of int:

```
type(True)
bool
```

```
type(False)
bool
```

A string is characters surrounded by quotation marks. You can use strings to represent a variety of text, with many different uses. The following is one example:

```
type("Hello")
str
```

Note

You will learn much more about strings and binary strings in Chapter 4.

A special type, NoneType, has only one value, None. It is used to represent something that has no value:

```
type(None)
NoneType
```

High-Level Versus Low-Level Languages

Writing software is, at its essence, just giving a computer instructions. The trick is to translate actions from a human-understandable form to instructions a computer can understand. Programming languages today range from being very close to how a computer understands logic to being much closer to human language. The languages closer to the computer's instructions are referred to as *low-level languages*. Machine code and assembly language are examples of low-level languages. With these languages, you have the ultimate control over exactly what your computer's processor does, but writing code with them is tedious and time-consuming.

Higher-level languages abstract groups of instructions together into larger chunks of functionality. Different languages across this spectrum have unique strengths. For example, the language C, which is on the lower end of high-level languages, enables you to directly manage a program's use of memory and write the highly optimized software required for embedded systems. Python, in contrast, is on the upper end of high-level languages. It does not allow you to directly say how much memory to use to save your data or free that memory when you're done. Python's syntax is much closer to logic as defined in human language and is generally easier to understand and write than low-level languages. Translating actions from human language to Python is generally a fast and intuitive process.

Statements

A Python program is constructed of statements. Each statement can be thought of as an action that the computer should perform. If you think of a software program as being akin to a recipe from a cookbook, a statement is a single instruction, such as "beat the eggs yolks until they turn white" or "bake for 15 minutes."

At the simplest, a Python statement is a single line of code with the end of the line signifying the end of the statement. A simple statement could, for example, call a single function, as in this expression statement:

```
print("hello")
```

A statement could also be more complicated, such as this statement, which evaluates conditions and assigns a variable based on that evaluation:

```
x,y = 5,6
bar = x**2 if (x < y) and (y or z) else x//2
```

Python allows for both simple and complex statements. Simple Python statements include expression, assert, assignment, pass, delete, return, yield, raise, break, continue, import, future, global, and nonlocal statements. This chapter covers some of these simple statements, and later chapters cover most of the rest of them. Chapter 5, "Execution Control," and Chapter 6, "Functions," cover complex statements.

Multiple Statements

While using a single statement is enough to define a program, most useful programs consist of multiple statements. The results of one statement can be used by the statements that follow, building functionality by combining actions. For example, you can use the following statement to assign a variable the result of an integer division, use that result to calculate a value for another variable, and then use both variables in a third statement as inputs to a `print` statement:

```
x = 23//3
y = x**2
print(f"x is {x}, y is {y}")
x is 7, y is 49
```

Expression Statements

A Python expression is a piece of code that evaluates to a value (or to None). This value could be, among other things, a mathematical expression or a call to a function or method. An expression statement is simply a statement that just has an expression but does not capture its output for further use. Expression statements are generally useful only in interactive environments, such as an IPython shell. In such an environment, the result of an expression is displayed to the user after it is run. This means that if you are in a shell and you want to know what a function returns or what 12344 divided by 12 is, you can see the output without coding a means to display it. You can also use an expression statement to see the value of a variable (as shown in the following example) or just to echo the display value of any type. Here are some simple expression statements and the output of each one:

```
23 * 42
966

"Hello"
'Hello'

import os
os.getcwd()
'/content'
```

You will see a number of expression statements used in this book to demonstrate Python functionality. In each case, you will see the expression first, with its result on the following line.

Assert Statements

An assert statement takes an expression as an argument and ensures that the result evaluates to True. Expressions that return False, None, zero, empty containers, and empty strings evaluate to False; all other values evaluate to True. (Containers are discussed in Chapter 3, "Sequences," and Chapter 4, "Other Data Structures.") An assert statement throws an error if the expression evaluates to False, as shown in this example:

```
assert(False)
```

```
------------------------------------------------------------
AssertionError              Traceback (most recent call last)
<ipython-input-5-8808c4021c9c> in <module>()
----> 1 assert(False)
```

Otherwise, the assert statement calls the expression and continues on to the next statement, as shown in this example:

```
assert(True)
```

You can use assert statements when debugging to ensure that some condition you assume to be true is indeed the case. These statements do have an impact on performance, though, so if you are using them generously when you develop, you might want to disable them when running your code in a production environment. If you are running your code from the command line, you can add the -o, optimize, flag to disable them:

```
python -o my_script.py
```

Assignment Statements

A variable is a name that points to some piece of data. It is important to understand that, in an assignment statement, the variable points to the data and is not the data itself. The same variable can be pointed to different items—even items that are of different types. In addition, you can change the data at which a variable points without changing the variable. As in the earlier examples in this chapter, a variable is assigned a value using the assignment operator (a single equals sign). The variable name appears to the left of the operator, and the value appears to the right. The following examples shows how to assign the value 12 to the variable x and the text 'Hello' to the variable y:

```
x = 12
y = 'Hello'
```

Once the variables are assigned values, you can use the variable names in place of the values. So, you can perform math by using the x variable or use the y variable to construct a larger piece of text, as shown in this example:

```
answer = x - 3
print(f"{y} Jeff, the answer is {answer}")
Hello Jeff, the answer is 9
```

You can see that the values for x and y are used where the variables have been inserted. You can assign multiple values to multiple variables in a single statement by separating the variable names and values with commas:

```
x, y, z = 1,'a',3.0
```

Here x is assigned the value 1, y the value 'a', and z the value 3.0.

It is a best practice to give your variables meaningful names that help explain their use. Using x for a value on the x-axis of a graph is fine, for example, but using x to hold the value for a client's first name is confusing; first_name would be a much clearer variable name for a client's first name.

Pass Statements

Pass statements are placeholders. They perform no action themselves, but when there is code that requires a statement to be syntactically correct, a pass statement can be used. A pass statement consists of the keyword `pass` and nothing else. Pass statements are generally used for stubbing out functions and classes when laying out code design (that is, putting in the names without functionality). You'll learn more about functions in Chapter 6, "Functions," and classes in Chapter 14.

Delete Statements

A delete statement deletes something from the running program. It consists of the `del` keyword followed by the item to be deleted, in parentheses. Once the item is deleted, it cannot be referenced again unless it is redefined. The following example shows a value being assigned to a variable and then deleted:

```
polly = 'parrot'
del(polly)
print(polly)
------------------------------------------------------------
NameError                    Traceback (most recent call last)
<ipython-input-6-c0525896ade9> in <module>()
      1 polly = 'parrot'
      2 del(polly)
----> 3 print(polly)

NameError: name 'polly' is not defined
```

When you try to access the variable using a `print` function in this example, an error is raised.

> **Note**
>
> Python has its own garbage collection system, and, generally you don't need to delete objects to free up memory, but there may be times when you want to remove them anyway.

Return Statements

A return statement defines the return value of a function. You will see how to write functions, including using return statements, in Chapter 6.

Yield Statements

Yield statements are used in writing generator functions, which provide a powerful way to optimize for performance and memory usage. We cover generators in Chapter 13, "Functional Programming."

Raise Statements

Some of the examples so far in this chapter have demonstrated code that causes errors. Such errors that occur during the running of a program (as opposed to errors in syntax that prevent a program from running at all) are called *exceptions*. Exceptions interrupt the normal execution of a program, and unless they are handled, cause the program to exit. Raise statements are used both to re-invoke an exception that has been caught and to raise either a built-in exception or an exception that you have designed specifically for your program. Python has many built-in exceptions, covering many different use cases (see https://docs.python.org/3/library/exceptions. html#bltin-exceptions). If you want to invoke one of these built-in exceptions, you can use a raise statement, which consists of the `raise` keyword followed by the exception. For example, `NotImplementedError` is an error used in class hierarchies to indicate that a child class should implement a method (see Chapter 14). The following example raises this error with a `raise` statement:

```
raise NotImplementedError
```
```
------------------------------------------------------------
NotImplementedError        Traceback (most recent call last)
<ipython-input-1-91639a24e592> in <module>()
----> 1 raise NotImplementedError
```

Break Statements

You use a break statement to end a loop before its normal looping condition is met. Looping and break statements are covered in Chapter 5.

Continue Statements

You use a continue statement to skip a single iteration of a loop. These statements are also covered in Chapter 5.

Import Statements

One of the most powerful features of writing software is the ability to reuse pieces of code in different contexts. Python code can be saved in files (with the .py extension); if these files are designed for reuse, they are referred to as *modules*. When you run Python, whether in an interactive session or as a standalone program, some features are available as core language features, which means you can use them directly, without additional setup. When you install Python, these core features are installed, and so is the Python Standard Library. This library is a series of modules that you can bring into your Python session to extend functionality. To have access to one of these modules in your code, you use an import statement, which consists of the keyword `import` and the name of the module to import. The following example shows how to import the os module, which is used to interact with the operating system:

```
import os
```

Once os is imported, you can use the module's functionality as if it were built in. The os module has a `listdir` function that lists the contents of the current directory:

```
os.listdir()
['.config', 'sample_data']
```

When modules or groups of modules are prepared for wider distribution, they are referred to as *packages*. One of the appealing aspects of Python, especially for data science, is the large ecosystem of third-party packages. These packages can be local to you or your organization, but the majority of public packages are hosted in the Python Package Index, pypi.org. To use one of these packages, you must install it first, generally by using `pip`, the standard package manager for Python. For example, to install the famously useful Pandas library for your local use, you run the following at the command line:

```
pip install pandas
```

Then you import it into your code:

```
import pandas
```

You can also give a module an alias during import. For example, it is a common convention to import Pandas as pd:

```
import pandas as pd
```

You can then reference the module by using the alias rather than the module name, as shown in this example:

```
pd.read_excel('/some_excel_file.xls')
```

You can also import specific parts of a module by using the `from` keyword with `import`:

```
import os from path
path
<module 'posixpath' from '/usr/lib/python3.6/posixpath.py'>
```

This example imports the submodule path from the module `os`. You can now use `path` in your program as if it were defined by your own code.

Future Statements

Future statements allow you to use certain modules that are part of a future release. This book does not cover them as they are rarely used in Data Science.

Global Statements

Scope in a program refers to the environment that shares definitions of names and values. Earlier you saw that when you define a variable in an assignment statement, that variable retains its name and value for future statements. These statements are said to share *scope*. When you start writing functions (in Chapter 6) and classes (in Chapter 14), you will encounter scopes that are not shared. Using a global statement is a way to share variables across scopes. (You will learn more about global statements in Chapter 13.)

Nonlocal Statements

Using nonlocal statements is another way of sharing variables across scope. Whereas a global variable is shared across a whole module, a nonlocal statement encloses the current scope. Nonlocal statements are valuable only with multiple nested scopes, and you should not need them outside of very specialized situations, so this book does not cover them.

Print Statements

When you are working in an interactive environment such as the Python shell, IPython, or, by extension, a Colab notebook, you can use expression statements to see the value of any Python expression. (An *expression* is piece of code that evaluates to a value.) In some cases, you may need to output text in other ways, such as when you run a program at the command line or in a cloud function. The most basic way to display output in such situations is to use a print statement. By default, the `print` function outputs text to the standard-out stream. You can pass any of the built-in types or most other objects as arguments to be printed. Consider these examples:

```
print(1)
1
```

```
print('a')
a
```

You can also pass multiple arguments, and they are printed on the same line:

```
print(1,'b')
1 b
```

You can use an optional argument to define the separator used between items when multiple arguments are provided:

```
print(1,'b',sep='->')
1->b
```

You can even print the `print` function itself:

```
print(print)
<built-in function print>
```

Performing Basic Math Operations

You can use Python as a calculator. Basic math operations are built into the core functionality. You can do math in an interactive shell or use the results of calculations in a program. The following are examples of addition, subtraction, multiplication, division, and exponentiation in Python:

```
2 + 3
5
```

```
5 - 6
-1
```

```
3*4
12
```

```
9/3
3.0
```

```
2**3
8
```

Notice that division returns a floating-point number, even if integers are used. If you want to limit the result of division to integers, you can use a doubled forward slash, as shown in this example:

```
5//2
2
```

Another handy operator is modulo, which returns the remainder of a division. To perform the modulo operation, you use the percent sign:

```
5%2
1
```

Modulo is useful in determining whether one number is a factor of another (in which case the result is zero). This example uses the `is` keyword to test if the result of the modulo is zero:

```
14 % 7 is 0
True
```

We will look at more math operations in Part II, "Data Science Libraries."

Using Classes and Objects with Dot Notation

In Chapter 14 you will learn about defining your own classes and objects. For now, you can think of an object as a bundling of functionality with data. The majority of things in Python have attributes or methods attached to them. To access an object's attributes or methods (that is, functions attached to an object), you use dot syntax. To access an attribute, simply use a dot after the object's name, followed by the attribute name.

The following example shows how to access the `numerator` attribute of an integer:

```
a_number = 2
a_number.numerator
```

You access object methods in a similar way, but with parentheses following. The following example uses the `to_bytes()` method of the same integer:

```
a_number.to_bytes(8, 'little')
b'\x02\x00\x00\x00\x00\x00\x00\x00'
```

Summary

Programming languages provide a means of translating human instructions to computer instructions. Python uses different types of statements to give a computer instructions, with each statement describing an action. You can combine statements together to create software. The data on which actions are taken is represented in Python by a variety of types, including both built-in types and types defined by developers and third parties. These types have their own characteristics, attributes, and, in many cases, methods that can be accessed using the dot syntax.

Questions

1. With Python, what is the output of `type(12)`?

2. When using Python, what is the effect of using `assert(True)` on the statements that follow it?

3. How would you use Python to invoke the exception `LastParamError`?

4. How would you use Python to print the string `"Hello"`?

5. How do you use Python to raise 2 to the power of 3?

3

Sequences

Errors using inadequate data are much less than those using no data at all.

Charles Babbage

In This Chapter

- Shared sequence operations
- Lists and tuples
- Strings and string methods
- Ranges

In Chapter 2, "Fundamentals of Python," you learned about collections of types. This chapter introduces the group of built-in types called *sequences*. A sequence is an ordered, finite collection. You might think of a sequence as a shelf in a library, where each book on the shelf has a location and can be accessed easily if you know its place. The books are ordered, with each book (except those at the ends) having books before and after it. You can add books to the shelf, and you can remove them, and it is possible for the shelf to be empty. The built-in types that comprise a sequence are lists, tuples, strings, binary strings, and ranges. This chapter covers the shared characteristics and specifics of these types.

Shared Operations

The sequences family shares quite a bit of functionality. Specifically, there are ways of using sequences that are applicable to most of the group members. There are operations that relate to sequences having a finite length, for accessing the items in a sequence, and for creating a new sequence based a sequence's content.

Testing Membership

You can test whether an item is a member of a sequence by using the in operation. This operation returns True if the sequence contains an item that evaluates as equal to the item in question, and it returns False otherwise. The following are examples of using in with different sequence types:

```
'first' in ['first', 'second', 'third']
True
```

```
23 in (23,)
True
```

```
'b' in 'cat'
False
```

```
b'a' in b'ieojjza'
True
```

You can use the keyword not in conjunction with in to check whether something is absent from a sequence:

```
'b' not in 'cat'
True
```

The two places you are most likely to use in and not in are in an interactive session to explore data and as part of an if statement (see Chapter 5, "Execution Control").

Indexing

Because a sequence is an ordered series of items, you can access an item in a sequence by using its position, or *index*. Indexes start at zero and go up to one less than the number of items. In an eight-item sequence, for example, the first item has an index of zero, and the last item an index of seven.

To access an item by using its index, you use square brackets around the index number. The following example defines a string and accesses its first and last substrings using their index numbers:

```
name = "Ignatius"
name[0]
'I'
```

```
name[4]
't'
```

You can also index counting back from the end of a sequence by using negative index numbers:

```
name[-1]
's'
```

```
name[-2]
'u'
```

Slicing

You can use indexes to create new sequences that represent subsequences of the original. In square brackets, supply the beginning and ending index numbers of the subsequence separated by a colon, and a new sequence is returned:

```
name = "Ignatius"
name[2:5]
'nat'
```

The subsequence that is returned contains items starting from the first index and up to, but not including, the ending index. If you leave out the beginning index, the subsequence starts at the beginning of the parent sequence; if you leave out the end index, the subsequence goes to the end of the sequence:

```
name[:5]
'Ignat'
```

```
name[4:]
'tius'
```

You can use negative index numbers to create slices counting from the end of a sequence. This example shows how to grab the last three letters of a string:

```
name[-3:]
'ius'
```

If you want a slice to skip items, you can provide a third argument that indicates what to count by. So, if you have a list sequence of integers, as shown earlier, you can create a slice just by using the starting and ending index numbers:

```
scores = [0, 1, 2, 3, 4, 5, 6, 7, 8, 9, 10, 11, 12, 13, 14, 15, 16, 17, 18]
scores[3:15]
[3, 4, 5, 6, 7, 8, 9, 10, 11, 12, 13, 14]
```

But you can also indicate the step to take, such as counting by threes:

```
scores[3:15:3]
[3, 6, 9, 12]
```

To count backward, you use a negative step:

```
scores[18:0:-4]
[18, 14, 10, 6, 2]
```

Interrogation

You can perform shared operations on sequences to glean information about them. Because a sequence is finite, it has a length, which you can find by using the len function:

```
name = "Ignatius"
len(name)
8
```

You can use the `min` and `max` functions to find the minimum and maximum items, respectively:

```
scores = [0, 1, 2, 3, 4, 5, 6, 7, 8, 9, 10, 11, 12, 13, 14, 15, 16, 17, 18]
min(scores)
0
```

```
max(name)
'u'
```

These methods assume that the contents of a sequence can be compared in a way that implies an ordering. For sequence types that allow for mixed item types, an error occurs if the contents cannot be compared:

```
max(['Free', 2, 'b'])
-----------------------------------------------------------------------
TypeError                          Traceback (most recent call last)
<ipython-input-15-d8babe38f9d9> in <module>()
----> 1 max(['Free', 2, 'b'])
TypeError: '>' not supported between instances of 'int' and 'str'
```

You can find out how many times an item appears in a sequence by using the count method:

```
name.count('a')
1
```

You can get the index of an item in a sequence by using the `index` method:

```
name.index('s')
7
```

You can use the result of the `index` method to create a slice up to an item, such as a letter in a string:

```
name[:name.index('u')]
'Ignati'
```

Math Operations

You can perform addition and multiplication with sequences of the same type. When you do, you conduct these operations on the sequence, not on its contents. So, for example, adding the list [1] to the list [2] will produce the list [1,2], not [3]. Here is an example of using the plus (+) operator to create a new string from three separate strings:

```
"prefix" + "-" + "postfix"
'prefix-postfix'
```

The multiplication (*) operator works by performing multiple additions on the whole sequence, not on its contents:

```
[0,2] * 4
[0, 2, 0, 2, 0, 2, 0, 2]
```

This is a useful way of setting up a sequence with default values. For example, say that you want to track scores for a set number of participants in a list. You can initialize that list so that it has an initial score for each participant by using multiplication:

```
num_participants = 10
scores = [0] * num_participants
scores
[0, 0, 0, 0, 0, 0, 0, 0, 0, 0]
```

Lists and Tuples

Lists and tuples are sequences that can hold objects of any type. Their contents can be of mixed types, so you can have strings, integers, instances, floats, and anything else in the same list. The items in lists and tuples are separated by commas. The items in a list are enclosed in square brackets, and the items in a tuple are enclosed in parentheses. The main difference between lists and tuples is that lists are mutable, and tuples are immutable. This means that you can change the contents of a list, but once a tuple is created, it cannot be changed. If you want to change the contents of a tuple, you need to make a new one based on the content of the current one. Because of the mutability difference, lists have more functionality than tuples—and they also use more memory.

Creating Lists and Tuples

You create a list by using the list constructor, list(), or by just using the square bracket syntax. To create a list with initial values, for example, simply supply the values in brackets:

```
some_list = [1,2,3]
some_list
[1, 2, 3]
```

You can create tuples by using the tuple constructor, tuple(), or using parentheses. If you want to create a tuple with a single item, you must follow that item with a comma, or Python will interpret the parentheses not as indicating a tuple but as indicating a logical grouping. You can also create a tuple without parentheses by just putting a comma after an item. Listing 3.1 provides examples of tuple creation.

Listing 3.1   **Creating Tuples**

```
tup = (1,2)
tup
(1,2)

tup = (1,)
tup
(1,)

tup = 1,2,
tup
(1,2)
```

> **Warning**
>
> A common but subtle bug occurs when you leave a trailing comma behind an argument to a function. It turns the argument into a tuple containing the original argument. So the second argument to the function `my_function(1, 2,)` will be `(2,)` and not 2.

You can also use the list or tuple constructors with a sequence as an argument. The following example uses a string and creates a list of the items the string contains:

```
name = "Ignatius"
letters = list(name)
letters
['I', 'g', 'n', 'a', 't', 'i', 'u', 's']
```

Adding and Removing List Items

You can add items to a list and remove items from a list. To conceptualize how it works, think of a list as a stack of books. The most efficient way to add items to a list is to use the append method, which adds an item to the end of the list, much as you could easily add a book to the top of a stack. To add an item to a different position in the list, you can use the `insert` method, with the index number where you wish to position the new item as an argument. This is less efficient than using the append method as the other items in the list may need to move to make room for the new item; however, this is typically an issue only in very large lists. Listing 3.2 shows examples of appending and inserting.

Listing 3.2 **Appending and Inserting List Items**

```
flavours = ['Chocolate', 'Vanilla']
flavours
['Chocolate', 'Vanilla']

flavours.append('SuperFudgeNutPretzelTwist')
flavours
['Chocolate', 'Vanilla', 'SuperFudgeNutPretzelTwist']

flavours.insert(0,"sourMash")
flavours
['sourMash', 'Chocolate', 'Vanilla', 'SuperFudgeNutPretzelTwist']
```

To remove an item from a list, you use the pop method. With no argument, this method removes the last item. By using an optional index argument, you can specify a specific item. In either case, the item is removed from the list and returned.

The following example pops the last item off the list and then pops off the item at index 0. You can see that both items are returned when they are popped and that they are then gone from the list:

```
flavours.pop()
'SuperFudgeNutPretzelTwist'
```

```
flavours.pop(0)
'sourMash'
```

```
flavours
['Chocolate', 'Vanilla']
```

To add the contents of one list to another, you use the `extend` method:

```
deserts = ['Cookies', 'Water Melon']
desserts
['Cookies', 'Water Melon']
```

```
desserts.extend(flavours)
desserts
['Cookies', 'Water Melon', 'Chocolate', 'Vanilla']
```

This method modifies the first list so that it now has the contents of the second list appended to its contents.

Nested List Initialization

There is a tricky bug that bites beginning Python developers. It involves combining list mutability with the nature of multiplying sequences. If you want to initialize a list containing four sublists, you might try multiplying a single list in a list like this:

```
lists = [[]] * 4
lists
[[], [], [], []]
```

This appears to have worked, until you modify one of the sublists:

```
lists[-1].append(4)
lists
[[4], [4], [4], [4]]
```

All of the sublists are modified! This is because the multiplication only initializes one list and references it four times. The references look independent until you try modifying one. The solution to this is to use a list comprehension (discussed further in Chapter 13, "Functional Programming"):

```
lists = [[] for _ in range(4)]
lists[-1].append(4)
lists
[[], [], [], [4]]
```

Unpacking

You can assign values to multiple variables from a list or tuple in one line:

```
a, b, c = (1,3,4)
a
1
```

```
b
3
```

```
c
4
```

Or, if you want to assign multiple values to one variable while assigning single ones to the others, you can use a * next to the variable that will take multiple values. Then that variable will absorb all the items not assigned to other variables:

```
*first, middle, last = ['horse', 'carrot', 'swan', 'burrito', 'fly']
first
['horse', 'carrot', 'swan']
```

```
last
'fly'
```

```
middle
'burrito'
```

Sorting Lists

For lists you can use built-in sort and reverse methods that can change the order of the contents. Much like the sequence min and max functions, these methods work only if the contents are comparable, as shown in these examples:

```
name = "Ignatius"
letters = list(name)
letters
['I', 'g', 'n', 'a', 't', 'i', 'u', 's']
```

```
letters.sort()
letters
['I', 'a', 'g', 'i', 'n', 's', 't', 'u']
```

```
letters.reverse()
letters
['u', 't', 's', 'n', 'i', 'g', 'a', 'I']
```

Strings

A string is a sequence of characters. In Python, strings are Unicode by default, and any Unicode character can be part of a string. Strings are represented as characters surrounded by quotation marks. Single or double quotations both work, and strings made with them are equal:

```
'Here is a string'
'Here is a string'
```

```
"Here is a string" == 'Here is a string'
True
```

If you want to include quotation marks around a word or words within a string, you need to use one type of quotation marks—single or double—to enclose that word or words and use the other type of quotation marks to enclose the whole string. The following example shows the word *is* enclosed in double quotation marks and the whole string enclosed in single quotation marks:

```
'Here "is" a string'
'Here "is" a string'
```

You enclose multiple-line strings in three sets of double quotation marks as shown in the following example:

```
a_very_large_phrase = """
Wikipedia is hosted by the Wikimedia Foundation,
a non-profit organization that also hosts a range of other projects.
"""
```

With Python strings you can use special characters, each preceded by a backslash. The special characters include \t for tab, \r for carriage return, and \n for newline. These characters are interpreted with special meaning during printing. While these characters are generally useful, they can be inconvenient if you are representing a Windows path:

```
windows_path = "c:\row\the\boat\now"
print(windows_path)
```

```
ow heoat
    ow
```

For such situations, you can use Python's raw string type, which interprets all characters literally. You signify the raw string type by prefixing the string with an r :

```
windows_path = r"c:\row\the\boat\now"
print(windows_path)
c:\row\the\boat\now
```

As demonstrated in Listing 3.3, there are a number of string helper functions that enable you to deal with different capitalizations.

Listing 3.3 **String Helper Functions**

```
captain = "Patrick Tayluer"
captain
'Patrick Tayluer'

captain.capitalize()
'Patrick tayluer'

captain.lower()
'patrick tayluer'

captain.upper()
'PATRICK TAYLUER'
```

```
captain.swapcase()
'pATRICK tAYLUER'

captain = 'patrick tayluer'
captain.title()
'Patrick Tayluer'
```

Python 3.6 introduced format strings, or f-strings. You can insert values into f-strings at runtime by using replacement fields, which are delimited by curly braces. You can insert any expression, including variables, into the replacement field. An f-string is prefixed with either an F or an f, as shown in this example:

```
strings_count = 5
frets_count = 24
f"Noam Pikelny's banjo has {strings_count} strings and {frets_count} frets"
'Noam Pikelny's banjo has 5 strings and 24 frets'
```

This example shows how to insert a mathematic expression into the replacement field:

```
a = 12
b = 32
f"{a} times {b} equals {a*b}"
'12 times 32 equals 384'
```

This example shows how to insert items from a list into the replacement field:

```
players = ["Tony Trischka", "Bill Evans", "Alan Munde"]
f"Performances will be held by {players[1]}, {players[0]}, and {players[2]}"
'Performances will be held by Bill Evans, Tony Trischka, and Alan Munde'
```

Ranges

Using range objects is an efficient way to represent a series of numbers, ordered by value. They are largely used for specifying the number of times a loop should run. Chapter 5 introduces loops. Range objects can take start (optional), end, and step (optional) arguments. Much as with slicing, the start is included in the range, and the end is not. Also as with slicing, you can use negative steps to count down. Ranges calculate numbers as you request them, and so they don't need to store more memory for large ranges. Listing 3.4 demonstrates how to create ranges with and without the optional arguments. This listing makes lists from the ranges so that you can see the full contents that the range would supply.

Listing 3.4 **Creating Ranges**

```
range(10)
range(0, 10)

list(range(1, 10))
[1, 2, 3, 4, 5, 6, 7, 8, 9]
```

```
list(range(0,10,2))
[0, 2, 4, 6, 8]

list(range(10, 0, -2))
[10, 8, 6, 4, 2]
```

Summary

This chapter covers the import group of types known as sequences. A sequence is an ordered, finite collection of items. Lists and tuples can contain mixed types. Lists can be modified after creation, but tuples cannot. Strings are sequences of text. Range objects are used to describe ranges of numbers. Lists, strings, and ranges are among the most commonly used types in Python.

Questions

1. How would you test whether a is in the list my_list?

2. How would you find out how many times b appears in a string named my_string?

3. How would you add a to the end of the list my_list?

4. Are the strings 'superior' and "superior" equal?

5. How would you make a range going from 3 to 13?

Other Data Structures

Statistical thinking will one day be as necessary for efficient citizenship as the ability to read and write.

Samuel S. Wilks

In This Chapter

- Creating dictionaries
- Accessing and updating dictionary contents
- Creating sets
- Set operations

The order-based representation of data is powerful, but other data representations are also possible. Dictionaries and sets are data structures that do not rely on the order of the data. Both are powerful models that are integral to the Python toolbox.

Dictionaries

Imagine that you are doing a study to determine if there is a correlation between student height and grade point average (GPA). You need a data structure to represent the data for an individual student, including the person's name, height, and GPA. You could store the information in a list or tuple. You would have to keep track of which index represented which piece of data, though. A better representation would be to label the data so that you wouldn't need to track the translation from index to attribute. You can use dictionaries to store data as key/value pairs. Every item, or value, in a dictionary is accessed using a key. This lookup is very efficient and is much faster than searching a long sequence.

With a key/value pair, the key and the value are separated with a colons. You can present multiple key/value pairs, separated by commas and enclosed in curly brackets. So, a dictionary for the student record might look like this:

```
{ 'name': 'Betty', 'height': 62,'gpa': 3.6 }
```

The keys for this dictionary are the strings 'name', 'height', and 'gpa'. Each key points to a piece of data: 'name' points to the string 'Betty', 'height' points to the integer 62, and 'gpa' points to the floating point number 3.6. The values can be of any type, though there are some restrictions on the key type, as discussed later in the chapter.

Creating Dictionaries

You can create dictionaries with or without initial data. You can create an empty dictionary by using the dict() constructor method or by simply using curly braces:

```
dictionary = dict()
dictionary
{}

dictionary = {}
dictionary
{}
```

The first example creates an empty dictionary by using the dict() constructor method and assigns that dictionary to a variable named dictionary. The second example creates an empty dictionary by using curly braces and also assigns to the same variable. Each of these examples produces an empty dictionary, represented by empty curly braces.

You can also create dictionaries initialized with data. One option for doing this is to pass in the keys and values as named parameters as in this example:

```
subject_1 = dict(name='Paula', height=64, gpa=3.8, ranking=1)
```

An alternative is to pass in the key/value pairs to the constructor as a list or tuple of lists or tuples, with each sublist being a key/value pair:

```
subject_2 = dict([['name','Paula'],['height',64],['gpa',3.8]],['ranking',1])
```

A third option is to create a dictionary by using curly braces, with the keys and values paired using colons and separated with commas:

```
subject_3 = {'name':'Paula', 'height':64, 'gpa':3.8, 'ranking':1}
```

These three methods all create dictionaries that evaluate the same way, as long as the same keys and values are used:

```
subject_1 == subject_2 == subject_3
True
```

Accessing, Adding, and Updating by Using Keys

Dictionary keys provide a means to access and change data. You generally access data by the relevant key in square brackets, in much the way you access indexes in sequences:

```
student_record = {'name':'Paula', 'height':64, 'gpa':3.8}
student_record['name']
'Paula'
```

```
student_record['height']
64
```

```
student_record['gpa']
3.8
```

If you want to add a new key/value pair to an existing dictionary, you can assign the value to the slot by using the same syntax:

```
student_record['applied'] = '2019-10-31'
student_record
{'name':'Paula',
 'height':64,
 'gpa':3.8,
 'applied': '2019-10-31'}
```

The new key/value pair is now contained in the original dictionary.

If you want to update the value for an existing key, you can also use the square bracket syntax:

```
student_record['gpa'] = 3.0
student_record['gpa']
3.0
```

A handy way to increment numeric data is by using the += operator, which is a shortcut for updating a value by adding to it:

```
student_record['gpa'] += 1.0
student_record['gpa']
4.0
```

Removing Items from Dictionaries

Sometimes you need to remove data, such as when a dictionary includes personally identifiable information (PII). Say that your data includes a student's ID, but this ID is irrelevant to a particular study. In order to preserve the privacy of the student, you could update the value for the ID to None:

```
student_record = {'advisor': 'Pickerson',
                  'first': 'Julia',
                  'gpa': 4.0,
                  'last': 'Brown',
                  'major': 'Data Science',
                  'minor': 'Math'}
student_record['id'] = None
student_record
{'advisor': 'Pickerson',
 'first': 'Julia',
 'gpa': 4.0,
 'id': None,
 'last': 'Brown',
 'major': 'Data Science',
 'minor': 'Math'}
```

This would prevent anyone from using the ID.

Another option would be to remove the key/value pair altogether by using the del() function. This function takes the dictionary with the key in square brackets as an argument and removes the appropriate key/value pair:

```
del(student_record['id'])
student_record
{'advisor': 'Pickerson',
 'first': 'Julia',
 'gpa': 4.0,
 'last': 'Brown',
 'major': 'Data Science',
 'minor': 'Math'}
```

> **Note**
> Of course, to really protect the subject's identity, you would want to remove the person's name as well as any other PII.

Dictionary Views

Dictionary views are objects that offer insights into a dictionary. There are three views: dict_keys, dict_values, and dict_items. Each view type lets you look at the dictionary from a different perspective.

Dictionaries have a keys() method, which returns a dict_keys object. This object gives you access to the current keys of the dictionary:

```
keys = subject_1.keys()
keys
dict_keys(['name', 'height', 'gpa', 'ranking'])
```

The values() method returns a dict_values object, which gives you access to the values stored in the dictionary:

```
values = subject_1.values()
values
dict_values(['Paula', 64, 4.0, 1])
```

The items() method returns a dict_items object, which represents the key/value pairs in a dictionary:

```
items = subject_1.items()
items
dict_items([('name', 'Paula'), ('height', 64), ('gpa', 4.0), ('ranking', 1)])
```

You can test membership in any of these views by using the in operator. This example shows how to check whether the key 'ranking' is used in this dictionary:

```
'ranking' in keys
True
```

This example shows how to check whether the integer 1 is one of the values in the dictionary:

```
1 in values
True
```

This example shows how to check whether the key/value pair mapping 'ranking' is 1:

```
('ranking',1) in items
True
```

Starting in Python 3.8, dictionary views are dynamic. This means that if you change a dictionary after acquiring a view, the view reflects the new changes. For example, say that you want to delete a key/value pair from the dictionary whose views are accessed above, as shown here:

```
del(subject_1['ranking'])
subject_1
{'name': 'Paula', 'height': 64, 'gpa': 4.0}
```

That key/value pair is also deleted from the view objects:

```
'ranking' in keys
False
```

```
1 in values
False
```

```
('ranking',1) in items
False
```

Every dictionary view type has a length, which you can access by using the same len function used with sequences:

```
len(keys)
3
```

```
len(values)
3
```

```
len(items)
3
```

As of Python 3.8, you can use the reversed function on a dict_key view to get a view in reverse order:

```
keys
dict_keys(['name', 'height', 'gpa'])
```

```
list(reversed(keys))
['gpa', 'height', 'name']
```

The dict_key views are set-like objects, which means that many set operations will work on them. This example shows how to create two dictionaries:

```
admission_record = {'first':'Julia',
                    'last':'Brown',
                    'id': 'ax012E4',
                    'admitted': '2020-03-14'}
```

```
student_record = {'first':'Julia',
                  'last':'Brown',
                  'id': 'ax012E4',
                  'gpa':3.8,
                  'major':'Data Science',
                  'minor': 'Math',
                  'advisor':'Pickerson'}
```

Then you can test the equality of keys:

```
admission_record.keys() == student_record.keys()
False
```

You can also look for a symmetric difference:

```
admission_record.keys() ^ student_record.keys()
{'admitted', 'advisor', 'gpa', 'major', 'minor'}
```

Here is how you look for intersection:

```
admission_record.keys() & student_record.keys()
{'first', 'id', 'last'}
```

Here is how you look for difference:

```
admission_record.keys() - student_record.keys()
{'admitted'}
```

Here is how you look for union:

```
admission_record.keys() | student_record.keys()
{'admitted', 'advisor', 'first', 'gpa', 'id', 'last', 'major', 'minor'}
```

Note

You will learn more about sets and set operations in the next section.

The most common use for key_item views is to iterate through a dictionary and perform an operation with each key/value pair. The following example uses a for loop (see Chapter 5, "Execution
Control") to print each pair:

```
for k,v in student_record.items():
    print(f"{k} => {v}")
first => Julia
last => Brown
gpa => 4.0
major => Data Science
minor => Math
advisor => Pickerson
```

You can do similar loops with dict_keys or dict_values, as required.

Checking to See If a Dictionary Has a Key

You can use the dict_key and the in operator to check whether a key is used in a dictionary:

```
'last' in student_record.keys()
True
```

As a shortcut, you can also test for a key without explicitly calling the dict_key view. Instead, you just use in directly with the dictionary:

```
'last' in student_record
True
```

This also works if you want to iterate through the keys of a dictionary. You don't need to access the dict_key view directly:

```
for key in student_record:
    print(f"key:  {key}")
 key: first
 key: last
 key: gpa
 key: major
 key: minor
 key: advisor
```

The get Method

Trying to access a key that is not in a dictionary by using the square bracket syntax causes an error:

```
student_record['name']
------------------------------------------------------------------------
KeyError                               Traceback (most recent call last)
<ipython-input-18-962c04650d3e> in <module>()
----> 1 student_record['name']
   KeyError: 'name'
```

This type of error stops the execution of a program that is run outside a notebook. One way to avoid these errors is to test whether the key is in the dictionary before accessing it:

```
if 'name' in student_record:
    student_record['name']
```

This example uses an if statement that accesses the key 'name' only if it is in the dictionary. (For more on if statements, see Chapter 5.)

As a convenience, dictionaries have a method, get(), that is designed to for safely accessing missing keys. By default, this method returns a None constant if the key is missing:

```
print( student_record.get('name') )
None
```

You can also provide a second argument, which is the value to return in the event of missing keys:

```
student_record.get('name', 'no-name')
'no-name'
```

You can also chain together multiple get statements:

```
student_record.get('name', admission_record.get('first', 'no-name'))
 'Julia'
```

This example tries to get the value for the key 'name' from the dictionary student_record, and if it is missing, it tries to get the value for the key 'first' from the dictionary admission_ record, and if that key is missing, it returns the default value 'no-name'.

Valid Key Types

You can change the values of some objects, but other objects have static values. The objects whose values can be changed are referred to as *mutable*. As you have already seen, lists are mutable objects; other objects whose value can be changed are also mutable. On the other hand, you cannot change the value of immutable objects. Immutable objects include integers, strings, range objects, binary strings, and tuples.

Immutable objects, with the exception of certain tuples, can be used as keys in dictionaries:

```
{ 1          : 'an integer',
  'string'   : 'a string',
  ('item',) : 'a tuple',
  range(12)  : 'a range',
  b'binary'  : 'a binary string' }
```

Mutable objects, such as lists, are not valid keys for dictionaries. If you try to use a list as a key, you experience an error:

```
{('item',): 'a tuple',
1: 'an integer',
b'binary': 'a binary string',
range(0, 12): 'a range',
'string': 'a string',
['a', 'list'] : 'a list key' }
```

```
    ---------------------------------------------------------------
    TypeError                             Traceback (most recent call last)
    <ipython-input-31-1b0e555de2b5> in <module>()
    ----> 1 { ['a', 'list'] : 'a list key' }
    TypeError: unhashable type: 'list'
```

A tuple whose contents are immutable can be used as a dictionary key. So, tuples of numbers, strings, and other tuples are all valid as keys:

```
tuple_key = (1, 'one', 1.0, ('uno',))
{ tuple_key: 'some value' }
{(1, 'one', 1.0, ('uno',)): 'some value'}
```

If a tuple contains a mutable object, such as a list, then the tuple is not a valid key:

```
bad_tuple = ([1, 2], 3)
{ bad_tuple: 'some value' }
---------------------------------------------------------------------------
TypeError                               Traceback (most recent call last)
<ipython-input-28-b2cddfdda91e> in <module>()
      1 bad_tuple = ([1, 2], 3)
----> 2 { bad_tuple: 'some value' }
TypeError: unhashable type: 'list'
```

The hash Method

You can think of a dictionary as storing values in an indexed list-like structure, with a method that quickly and reliably maps the key objects to the appropriate index numbers. This method is known as a hash function and can be found on immutable Python objects as the __hash__() method. It is designed to be used behind the scenes but can be called directly:

```
a_string = 'a string'
a_string.__hash__()
4815474858255585337

a_tuple = 'a','b',
a_tuple.__hash__()
7273358294597481374

a_number = 13
a_number.__hash__()
13
```

This hash function uses the value of an object to produce a consistent output. Hence for a mutable object, no consistent hash can be produced. You cannot get a hash of a mutable object such as a list:

```
a_list = ['a','b']
a_list.__hash__()
---------------------------------------------------------------------------
TypeError Traceback (most recent call last) <ipython-input-40-c4f99d4ea902> in
<module>()
      1 a_list = ['a','b']
----> 2 a_list.__hash__()
TypeError: 'NoneType' object is not callable
```

Dictionaries and lists are among the most commonly used data structures in Python. They give you great ways to structure data for meaningful, fast lookups.

> **Note**
>
> Although the key/value lookup mechanism does not rely on an order of the data, as of Python 3.7, the order of the keys reflects the order in which they were inserted.

Sets

The Python set data structure is an implementation of the sets you may be familiar with from mathematics. A *set* is an unordered collection of unique items. You can think of a set as a magic bag that does not allow duplicate objects. The items in sets can be any hashable type.

A set is represented in Python as a list of comma-separated items enclosed in curly braces:

```
{ 1, 'a', 4.0 }
```

You can create a set either by using the set() constructor or by using curly braces directly. However, when you use empty curly braces, you create an empty dictionary, not an empty set. If you want to create an empty set, you must use the set() constructor:

```
empty_set = set()
empty_set
set()
```

```
empty_set = {}
empty_set
{}
```

You can create a set with initial values by using either the constructor or the curly braces.

You can provide any type of sequence as the argument, and a set will be returned based on the unique items from the sequence:

```
letters = 'a', 'a', 'a', 'b', 'c'
unique_letters = set(letters)
unique_letters
{'a', 'b', 'c'}
```

```
unique_chars = set('mississippi')
unique_chars
{'i', 'm', 'p', 's'}
```

```
unique_num = {1, 1, 2, 3, 4, 5, 5}
unique_num
{1, 2, 3, 4, 5}
```

Much like dictionary keys, sets hash their contents to determine uniqueness. Therefore, the contents of a set must be hashable and, hence, immutable. A list cannot be a member of a set:

```
bad_set = { ['a','b'], 'c' }
---------------------------------------------------------------------------
TypeError                                 Traceback (most recent call last)
    <ipython-input-12-1179bc4af8b8> in <module>()
----> 1 bad_set = { ['a','b'], 'c' }
TypeError: unhashable type: 'list'
```

You can add items to a set by using the add() method:

```
unique_num.add(6)
unique_num
{1, 2, 3, 4, 5, 6}
```

You can use the `in` operator to test membership in a set:

```
3 in unique_num
True
```

```
3 not in unique_num
False
```

You can use the `len()` function to see how many items a set contains:

```
len(unique_num)
6
```

As with lists, you can remove and return an item from a set by using the `pop()` method:

```
unique_num.pop()
unique_num
{2, 3, 4, 5, 6}
```

Unlike with lists, you cannot rely on `pop()` to remove a set's items in any particular order. If you want to remove a particular item from a set, you can use the `remove()` method:

```
students = {'Karl', 'Max', 'Tik'}
students.remove('Karl')
students
{'Max', 'Tik'}
```

This method does not return the item removed. If you try to remove an item that is not found in the set, you get an error:

```
students.remove('Barb')
--------------------------------------------------------------------------
KeyError                                    Traceback (most recent call last)
    <ipython-input-3-a36a5744ac05> in <module>()
----> 1 students.remove('Barb')
KeyError: 'Barb'
```

You could write code to test whether an item is in a set before removing it, but there is a convenience function, `discard()`, that does not throw an error when you attempt to remove a missing item:

```
students.discard('Barb')
students.discard('Tik')
students
{'Max'}
```

You can remove all of the contents of a set by using the `clear()` method:

```
students.clear()
students
set()
```

Remember that because sets are unordered, they do not support indexing:

```
unique_num[3]
```

```
TypeError                            Traceback (most recent call last)
<ipython-input-16-fecab0cd5f95> in <module>()
----> 1 unique_num[3]
TypeError: 'set' object does not support indexing
```

You can test equality by using the equals, ==, and not equals, !=, operators (which are discussed in Chapter 5). Because sets are unordered, sets created from sequences with the same items in different orders are equal:

```
first = {'a','b','c','d'}
second = {'d','c','b','a'}
first == second
True

first != second
False
```

Set Operations

You can perform a number of operations with sets. Many set operations are offered both as methods on the set objects and as separate operators (<, <=, >, >=, &, |, and ^). The set methods can be used to perform operations between sets and other sets, and they can also be used between sets and other iterables (that is, data types that can be iterated over). The set operators work only between sets and other sets (or frozensets).

Disjoint

Two sets are disjoint if they have no items in common. With Python sets, you can use the disjoint() method to test this. If you test a set of even numbers against a set of odd numbers, they share no numbers, and hence the result of disjoint() is True:

```
even = set(range(0,10,2))
even
{0, 2, 4, 6, 8}

odd = set(range(1,11,2))
odd
{1, 3, 5, 7, 9}

even.isdisjoint(odd)
True
```

Subset

If all the items in a set, Set B, can be found in another set, Set A, then Set B is a subset of Set A. The subset() method tests whether the current set is a subset of another. The following example tests whether a set of positive multiples of 3 below 21 are a subset of positive integers below 21:

```
nums = set(range(21))
nums
{0, 1, 2, 3, 4, 5, 6, 7, 8, 9, 10, 11, 12, 13, 14, 15, 16, 17, 18, 19, 20}

threes = set(range(3,21,3))
threes
{3, 6, 9, 12, 15, 18}

threes.issubset(nums)
        True
```

You can use the <= operator to test whether a set to the left is a subset of a set to the right:

```
threes <= nums
True
```

As mentioned earlier in this chapter, the method version of this operator works with non-set arguments. The following example tests whether a set of multiples of 3 are in the range 0 through 20:

```
threes.issubset(range(21))
True
```

The operator does not work with a non-set object:

```
threes <= range(21)
--------------------------------------------------------------------------
TypeError                              Traceback (most recent call last)
    <ipython-input-30-dbd51effe302> in <module>()
    ----> 1 threes <= range(21)
TypeError: '<=' not supported between instances of 'set' and 'range'
```

Proper Subsets

If all the items of a set are contained in a second set, but not all the items in the second set are in the first set, then the first set is a proper subset of the second set. This is equivalent to saying that the first set is a subset of the second and that they are not equal. You use the < operator to test for proper subsets:

```
threes < nums
True

threes < {'3','6','9','12','15','18'}
False
```

Supersets and Proper Supersets

A superset is the reverse of a subset: If a set contains all the elements of another set, it is a subset of the second set. Similarly, if a set is a superset of another set and they are not equal, then it is a proper superset. Python sets have an issuperset() method, which takes another set or any other iterable as an argument:

```
nums.issuperset(threes)
True
```

```
nums.issuperset([1,2,3,4])
True
```

You use the greater-than-or-equal-to operator, >=, to test for supersets and the greater-than operator, >, to test for proper supersets:

```
nums >= threes
True
```

```
nums > threes
True
```

```
nums >= nums
True
```

```
nums > nums
False
```

Union

The union of two sets results in a set containing all the items in both sets. For Python sets you can use the union() method, which works with sets and other iterables, and the standalone bar operator, |, which returns the union of two sets:

```
odds = set(range(0,12,2))
odds
{0, 2, 4, 6, 8, 10}
```

```
evens = set(range(1,13,2))
evens
{1, 3, 5, 7, 9, 11}
```

```
odds.union(evens)
{0, 1, 2, 3, 4, 5, 6, 7, 8, 9, 10, 11}
```

```
odds.union(range(0,12))
{0, 1, 2, 3, 4, 5, 6, 7, 8, 9, 10, 11}
```

```
odds | evens
{0, 1, 2, 3, 4, 5, 6, 7, 8, 9, 10, 11}
```

Intersection

The intersection of two sets is a set containing all items shared by both sets. You can use the intersection() method or the and operator, &, to perform intersections:

```
under_ten = set(range(10))
odds = set(range(1,21,2))
under_ten.intersection(odds)
{1, 3, 5, 7, 9}
```

```
under_ten & odds
{1, 3, 5, 7, 9}
```

Difference

The difference between two sets is all of the items in the first set that are not in the second set. You can use the difference() method or the minus operator, –, to perform set difference:

```
odds.difference(under_ten)
{11, 13, 15, 17, 19}
```

```
odds - under_ten
{11, 13, 15, 17, 19}
```

Symmetric Difference

The symmetric difference of two sets is a set containing any items contained in only one of the original sets. Python sets have a symmetric_difference() method, and the caret operator, ^, for calculating the symmetric difference:

```
under_ten = set(range(10))
over_five = set(range(5, 15))
under_ten.symmetric_difference(over_five)
{0, 1, 2, 3, 4, 10, 11, 12, 13, 14}
```

```
under_ten ^ over_five
{0, 1, 2, 3, 4, 10, 11, 12, 13, 14}
```

Updating Sets

Python sets offer a number of ways to update the contents of a set in place. In addition to using update(), which adds the contents to a set, you can use variations that update based on the various set operations.

The following example shows how to update from another set:

```
unique_num = {0, 1, 2}
unique_num.update( {3, 4, 5, 7} )
unique_num
{0, 1, 2, 3, 4, 5, 7}
```

The following example shows how to update from a list:

```
unique_num.update( [8, 9, 10] )
unique_num
{0, 1, 2, 3, 4, 5, 7, 8, 9, 10}
```

The following example shows how to update the difference from a range:

```
unique_num.difference_update( range(0,12,2) )
unique_num
{1, 3, 5, 7, 9}
```

The following example shows how to update the intersection:

```
unique_num.intersection_update( { 2, 3, 4, 5 } )
unique num
{3, 5}
```

The following example shows how to update the symmetric difference:

```
unique_num.symmetric_difference_update( {5, 6, 7 } )
unique_num
{3, 6, 7}
```

The following example shows how to update the union operator:

```
unique_letters = set("mississippi")
unique_letters
{'i', 'm', 'p', 's'}
```

```
unique_letters |= set("Arkansas")
unique_letters
{'A', 'a', 'i', 'k', 'm', 'n', 'p', 'r', 's'}
```

The following example shows how to update the difference operator:

```
unique_letters -= set('Arkansas')
unique_letters
{'i', 'm', 'p'}
```

The following example shows how to update the intersection operator:

```
unique_letters &= set('permanent')
unique_letters
{'m', 'p'}
```

```
unique_letters ^= set('mud')  2 unique_letters
{'d', 'p', 'u'}
```

Frozensets

Because sets are mutable, they cannot be used as dictionary keys or even as items in sets. In Python, frozensets are set-like objects that are immutable. You can use frozensets in place of sets for any operation that does not change its contents, as in these examples:

```
froze = frozenset(range(10))
froze
frozenset({0, 1, 2, 3, 4, 5, 6, 7, 8, 9})

froze < set(range(21))
True

froze & set(range(5, 15))
frozenset({5, 6, 7, 8, 9})

froze ^ set(range(5, 15))
frozenset({0, 1, 2, 3, 4, 10, 11, 12, 13, 14})

froze | set(range(5,15))
frozenset({0, 1, 2, 3, 4, 5, 6, 7, 8, 9, 10, 11, 12, 13, 14})
```

Summary

Python's built-in data structures offer a variety of ways to represent and organize your data. Dictionaries and sets are both complements to the sequence types. Dictionaries map keys to values in an efficient way. Sets implement mathematical set operations as data structures. Both dictionaries and sets are great choices where order is not the best operating principle.

Questions

1. What are three ways to create a dictionary with the following key/value pairs:

   ```
   {'name': 'Smuah', 'height':62}
   ```

2. How would you update the value associated with the key gpa in the dictionary student to be '4.0'?

3. Given the dictionary data, how would you safely access the value for the key settings if that key might be missing?

4. What is the difference between a mutable object and immutable object?

5. How would you create a set from the string "lost and lost again"?

Execution Control

An approximate answer to the right problem is worth a good deal more than an exact answer to an approximate problem.

John Tukey

In This Chapter

- Introduction to compound statements
- Equality operations
- Comparison operations
- Boolean operations
- `if` statements
- `while` loops
- `for` loops

Up until this point in the book, you've seen statements as individual units, executing sequentially one line at a time. Programming becomes much more powerful and interesting when you can group statements together so that they execute as a unit. Simple statements that are joined together can perform more complex behaviors.

Compound Statements

Chapter 2, "Fundamentals of Python," introduces simple statements, each of which performs an action. This chapter looks at compound statements, which allow you to control the execution of a group of statements. This execution can occur only when a condition is true. The compound statements covered in this chapter include `for` loops, `while` loops, `if` statements, `try` statements, and `with` statements.

Compound Statement Structure

A compound statement consists of a controlling statement or statements and a group of statements whose execution is controlled. A control statement starts with a keyword indicating the type of compound statement, an expression specific to the type of statement, and then a colon:

```
<keyword> <expression>:
```

The controlled statements can be grouped in one of two ways. The first, more common, way is to group them as a *code block*, which is a group of statements that are run together. In Python, code blocks are defined using indentation. A group of statements that share the same indentation are grouped into the same code block. The group ends when there is a statement that is not indented as far as the others. That final statement is not part of the code block and will execute regardless of the control statement. This is what a code block looks like:

```
<control statement>:
    <controlled statement 1>
    <controlled statement 2>
    <controlled statement 3>
< statement ending block>
```

Using indentation to define code blocks is one of the features that differentiates Python from most other popular languages, which use other mechanisms, such as curly brackets, to group code.

Another way to group controlled statements is to list them directly following the control statement and separate the controlled statements with semicolons:

```
<control statement>:<controlled statement 1>;<controlled statement 2>;
```

You should use this second style only when you have very few controlled statements and you feel that limiting the compound statement to one line will enhance, not detract from, the readability of the program.

Evaluating to True or False

if statements, while loops, and for loops are all compound statement that rely on a controlling expression that must evaluate to True or False. Luckily, in Python, pretty much everything evaluates as equal to one of these. The four most commonly used built-in expressions used as controls for compound statements are equality operations, comparison operations, Boolean operations, and object evaluation.

Equality Operations

Python offers the equality operator, ==, the inequality operator, !=, and the identity operator, is. The equality and inequality operators both compare the value of two objects and return one of the constants True or False. Listing 5.1 assigns two variables with integer values of 1, and another with the value 2. It then uses the equality operator to show that the first two variables are equal, and the third is not. It does the same with the inequality operator, whose results are opposite those of the equality operator with the same inputs.

Listing 5.1 **Equality Operations**

```
# Assign values to variables
a, b, c = 1, 1, 2
# Check if value is equal
a == b
True

a == c
False

a != b
False

a != c
True
```

You can compare different types of objects by using the equality/inequality operators. For numeric types, such as floats and integers, the values are compared. For example, if you compare the integer 1 to the float 1.0, they evaluate as equal:

```
1 == 1.0
True
```

Most other cross-type comparisons return False, regardless of value. Comparing a string to an integer will always return False, regardless of the values:

```
'1' == 1
False
```

Web forms often report all user input as strings. A common problem occurs when trying to compare user input from a web form that represents a number but is of type string with an actual number. String input always evaluates to False when compared to a number, even if the input is a string version of the same value.

Comparison Operations

You use comparison operators to compare the order of objects. What "the order" means depends on the type of objects compared. For numbers, the comparison is the order on a number line, and for strings, the Unicode value of the characters is used. The comparison operators are less than (<), less than or equal to (<=), greater than (>), and greater than or equal to (>=). Listing 5.2 demonstrates the behavior of various comparison operators.

Listing 5.2 **Comparison Operations**

```
a, b, c = 1, 1, 2
a < b
False
```

```
a < c
True

a <= b
True

a > b
False

a >= b
True
```

There are certain cases where you can use comparison operators between objects of different types, such as with the numeric types, but most cross-type comparisons are not allowed. If you use a comparison operator with noncomparable types, such as a string and a list, an error occurs.

Boolean Operations

The Boolean operators are based on Boolean math, which you may have studied in a math or philosophy course. These operations were first formalized by the mathematician George Boole in the 19th century. In Python, the Boolean operators are and, or, and not. The and and or operators each take two arguments; the not operator takes only one.

The and operator evaluates to True if both of its arguments evaluate to True; otherwise, it evaluates to False. The or operator evaluates to True if either of its arguments evaluates to True; otherwise, it evaluates to False. The not operator returns True if its argument evaluates to False; otherwise, it evaluates to False. Listing 5.3 demonstrates these behaviors.

Listing 5.3 **Boolean Operations**

```
True and True
True

True and False
False

True or False
True

False or False
False

not False
True

not True
False
```

Both the and and or operators are short-circuit operators. This means they will only evaluate their input expression as much as is needed to determine the output. For example, say that you have two methods, `returns_false()` and `returns_true()`, and you use them as inputs to the and operator as follows:

```
returns_false() and returns_true()
```

If `returns_false()` returns `False`, `returns_true()` will not be called, as the result of the and operation is already determined. Similarly, say that you use them as arguments to the or operation, like this:

```
returns_true() or returns_false()
```

In this case, the second method will not be called if the first returns `True`.

The not operator always returns one of the Boolean constants `True` or `False`. The other two Boolean operators return the result of the last expression evaluated. This is very useful with object evaluation.

Object Evaluation

All objects in Python evaluate to `True` or `False`. This means you can use objects as arguments to Boolean operations. The objects that evaluate to `False` are the constants `None` and `False`, any numeric with a value of zero, or anything with a length of zero. This includes empty sequences, such as an empty string (`""`) or an empty list (`[]`). Almost anything else evaluates to `True`.

Because the or operator returns the last expression it evaluates, you can use it to create a default value when a variable evaluates to `False`:

```
a = ''
b = a or 'default value'
b
'default value'
```

Because this example assigns the first variable to an empty string, which has a length of zero, this variable evaluates to `False`. The or operator evaluates this and then evaluates and returns the second expression.

if Statements

The if statement is a compound statement. if statements let you branch the behavior of your code depending on the current state. You can use an if statement to take an action only when a chosen condition is met or use a more complex one to choose among multiple actions, depending on multiple conditions. The control statement starts with the keyword if followed by an expression (which evaluates to `True` or `False`) and then a colon. The controlled statements follow either on the same line separated by semicolons:

```
if True:message="It's True!";print(message)
It's True!
```

or as an indented block of code, separated by newlines:

```
if True:
    message="It's True"
    print(message)
It's True
```

In both of these examples, the controlling expression is simply the reserved constant True, which always evaluates to True. There are two controlled statements: The first assigns a string to the variable message, and the second prints the value of this variable. It's usually more readable to use the block syntax, as in the second example.

If the controlling expression evaluates to False, the program continues executing and skips the controlled statement(s):

```
if False:
    message="It's True"
    print(message)
```

The Walrus Operator

When you assign a value to a variable, Python does not return a value. A common situation is to make a variable assignment and then check the value of the variable. For example, you might assign to a variable the value returned by a function, and if that value is not None, you may use the returned object. The search method of the Python re module (covered in Chapter 15, "Other Topics") returns a match object if it finds a match in a string, and it returns None otherwise, so if you want to use the match object, you need to make sure it's not None first:

```
import re
s = '2020-12-14'
match = re.search(r'(\d\d\d\d)-(\d\d)-(\d\d)', s)
if match:
    print(f"Matched items: {match.groups(1)}")
else:
    print(f"No match found in {s}")
```

Python 3.8 introduced a new operator, the assignment operator (:=). It is referred to as the *walrus operator* due to its resemblance to a walrus's head. This operator assigns a value to a variable and returns that value. You could rewrite the match example by using it:

```
import re
s = '2020-12-14'
if match := re.search(r'(\d\d\d\d)-(\d\d)-(\d\d)', s):
    print(f"Matched items: {match.groups(1)}")
else:
    print(f"No match found in {s}")
```

This operator creates less complicated, more readable code.

Here is an example that uses a membership test as the controlling expression:

```
snack = 'apple'
fruit = {'orange', 'apple', 'pear'}
if snack in fruit:
    print(f"Yeah, {snack} is good!"
Yeah, apple is good!
```

This example checks whether the value of the variable snack is in the set fruit. If it is, an encouraging message is printed.

If you want to run an alternative block of code when the controlling expression is False, you can use an else statement. An else statement consists of the keyword else followed by a colon and then a block of code that will execute only if the controlling expression preceding it evaluates to False. This lets you branch the logic in your code. Think of it as choosing which actions to take based on the current state. Listing 5.4 shows an else statement added to the snack-related if statement. The second print statement executes only if the controlling expression snack in fruit is False.

Listing 5.4 **else Statements**

```
snack = 'cake'
fruit = {'orange', 'apple', 'pear'}
if snack in fruit:
    print(f"Yeah, {snack} is good!")
else:
    print(f"{snack}!? You should have some fruit")
cake!? You should have some fruit
```

If you want to have multiple branches in your code, you can nest if and else statements as shown in Listing 5.5. In this case, three choices are made: one if the balance is positive, one if it is negative, and one if it is negative.

Listing 5.5 **Nested else Statements**

```
balance = 2000.32
account_status = None

if balance > 0:
    account_status = 'Positive'
else:
    if balance == 0:
        account_status = 'Empty'
    else:
        account_status = 'Overdrawn'

print(account_status)
Positive
```

While this code is legitimate and will work the way it is supposed to, it is a little hard to read. To perform the same branching logic in a more concise way, you can use an elif statement. This type of statement is added after an initial if statement. It has a controlling expression of its own, which will be evaluated only if the previous statement's expression evaluates to False. Listing 5.6 performs the same logic as Listing 5.5, but has the nested else and if statements replaced by elif.

Listing 5.6 **elif Statements**

```
balance = 2000.32
account_status = None

if balance > 0:
    account_status = 'Positive'
elif balance == 0:
    account_status = 'Empty'
else:
    account_status = 'Overdrawn'


print(account_status)
Positive
```

By chaining multiple elif statements with an if statement, as demonstrated in Listing 5.7, you can perform complicated choices. Usually an else statement is added at the end to catch the case that all the controlling expressions are False.

Listing 5.7 **Chaining elif Statements**

```
fav_num = 13

if fav_num in (3,7):
    print(f"{fav_num} is lucky")
elif fav_num == 0:
    print(f"{fav_num} is evocative")
elif fav_num > 20:
    print(f"{fav_num} is large")
elif fav_num == 13:
    print(f"{fav_num} is my favorite number too")
else:
    print(f"I have no opinion about {fav_num}")
is my favorite number too
```

while **Loops**

A while loop consists of the keyword while followed by a controlling expression, a colon, and then a controlled code block. The controlled statement in a while loop executes only if the controlling statement evaluates to True; in this way, it is like an if statement. Unlike an if statement, however, the while loop repeatedly continues to execute the controlled block as long as its control statement remains True. Here is a while loop that executes as long as the variable counter is below five:

```
counter = 0
while counter < 5:
    print(f"I've counted {counter} so far, I hope there aren't more")
    counter += 1
```

Notice that the variable is incremented with each iteration. This guarantees that the loop will exit. Here is the output from running this loop:

```
I've counted 0 so far, I hope there aren't more
I've counted 1 so far, I hope there aren't more
I've counted 2 so far, I hope there aren't more
I've counted 3 so far, I hope there aren't more
I've counted 4 so far, I hope there aren't more
```

You can see that the loop runs five times, incrementing the variable each time.

> **Note**
> It is important to provide an exit condition, or your loop will repeat infinitely.

for Loops

for loops are used to iterate through some group of objects. This group can be a sequence, a generator, a function, or any other object that is iterable. An iterable object is any object that returns a series of items one at a time. for loops are commonly used to perform a block of code a set number of times or perform an action on each member of a sequence. The controlling statement of a for loop consists of the keyword for, a variable, the keyword in, and the iterable followed by a colon:

```
for <variable> in <iterable>:
```

The variable is assigned the first value from the iterable, the controlled block is executed with that value, and then the variable is assigned the next value. This continues as long as the iterable has values to return.

A common way to run a block of code a set number of times is to use a for loop with a range object as the iterable:

```
for i in range(6):
    j = i + 1
    print(j)
        1
        2
        3
        4
        5
        6
```

This example assigns the values 0, 1, 2, 3, 4, and 5 to the variable i, running a code block for each one.

Here is an example of using a list as the iterable:

```
colors = ["Green", "Red", "Blue"]
for color in colors:
    print(f"My favorite color is {color}")
    print("No, wait...")
My favorite color is Green
No, wait...
My favorite color is Red
No, wait...
My favorite color is Blue
No, wait...
```

Each item in the list is used in the code block, and when there are no items left, the loop exits.

break and continue Statements

The break statement gives you an early exit from a while or for loop. When the statement is evaluated, the current block ceases to execute, and the loop is ended. This is usually used in conjunction with a nested if statement. Listing 5.8 shows a loop whose controlling expression is always True. A nested if statement calls break when its condition is met, ending the loop at that point.

Listing 5.8   **break Statement**

```
fish = ['mackerel', 'salmon', 'pike']
beasts = ['salmon', 'pike', 'bear', 'mackerel']
i = 0

while True:
    beast = beasts[i]
    if beast not in fish:
        print(f"Oh no! It's not a fish, it's a {beast}")
        break
    print(f"I caught a {beast} with my fishing net")
    i += 1
I caught a salmon with my fishing net
I caught a pike with my fishing net
Oh no! It's not a fish, it's a bear
```

The continue statement skips a single iteration of a loop when it is invoked. It is also usually used in conjunction with a nested if statement. Listing 5.9 demonstrates the use of a continue statement to skip printing names that don't begin with the letter *b*.

Listing 5.9 `continue` **Statement**

```
for name in ['bob', 'billy', 'bonzo', 'fred', 'baxter']:
    if not name.startswith('b'):
            continue
    print(f"Fine fellow that {name}")
Fine fellow that bob
Fine fellow that billy
Fine fellow that bonzo
Fine fellow that baxter
```

Summary

Compound statements such as `if` statements, `while` loops, and `for` loops are a fundamental part of code beyond simple scripts. With the ability to branch and repeat your code, you can form blocks of action that describe complex behavior. You now have tools to structure more complex software.

Questions

1. What is printed by the following code if the variable a is set to an empty list?

   ```
   if a:
           print(f"Hiya {a}")
   else:
           print(f"Biya {a}")
   ```

2. What is printed by the previous code if the variable a is set to the string "Henry"?

3. Write a `for` loop that prints the numbers from 0 to 9, skipping 3, 5, and 7.

6

Functions

In our lust for measurement, we frequently measure that which we can rather than that which we wish to measure...and forget that there is a difference.

George Udny Yule

In This Chapter

- Defining functions
- Docstrings
- Positional and keyword parameters
- Wildcard parameters
- Return statements
- Scope
- Decorators
- Anonymous functions

The last and perhaps most powerful compound statement that we discuss is the function. Functions give you a way to name a code block wrapped as an object. That code can then be invoked by use of that name, allowing the same code to be called multiple times and in multiple places.

Defining Functions

A function definition defines a function object, which wraps the executable block. The definition does not run the code block but just defines the function. The definition describes how the function can be called, what it is named, what parameters can be passed to it, and what will be executed when it is invoked. The building blocks of a function are the controlling statement, an optional docstring, the controlled code block, and a return statement.

Control Statement

The first line of a function definition is the control statement, which takes the following form:

```
def <Function Name> (<Parameters>):
```

The def keyword indicates a function definition, <Function Name> is where the name that will be used to call the function is defined, and <Parameters> is where any arguments that can be passed to the function are defined. For example, the following function is defined with the name do_nothing and a single parameter named not_used:

```
def do_nothing(not_used):
    pass
```

The code block in this case consists of a single pass statement, which does nothing. The Python style guide, PEP8, has conventions for naming functions (see https://www.python.org/dev/peps/pep-0008/#function-and-variable-names).

Docstrings

The next part of a function definition is the documentation string, or *docstring*, which contains documentation for the function. It can be omitted, and the Python compiler will not object. However, it is highly recommended to supply a docstring for all but the most obvious methods. The docstring communicates your intentions in writing a function, what the function does, and how it should be called. PEP8 provides guidance regarding the content of docstrings (see https://www.python.org/dev/peps/pep-0008/#documentation-strings). The docstring consists of a single-line string or a multiline string surrounded in three pairs of double quotes that immediately follows the control statement:

```
def do_nothing(not_used):
    """This function does nothing."""
    pass
```

For a single-line docstring, the quotes are on the same line as the text. For a multiline docstring, the quotes are generally above and below the text, as in Listing 6.1.

Listing 6.1   **Multiline Docstring**

```
def do_nothing(not_used):
    """
    This function does nothing.
    This function uses a pass statement to
    avoid doing anything.
    Parameters:
        not_used - a parameter of any type,
                   which is not used.
    """
    pass
```

The first line of the docstring should be a statement summarizing what the function does. With a more detailed explanation, a blank line is left after the first statement. There are many different possible conventions for what is contained after the first line of a docstring, but generally you want to offer an explanation of what the function does, what parameters it takes, and what it is expected to return. The docstring is useful both for someone reading your code and for various utilities that read and display either the first line or the whole docstring. For example, if you call the help() function on the function do_nothing(), the docstring is displayed as shown in Listing 6.2.

Listing 6.2   **Docstring from help**

```
help(do_nothing)
Help on function do_nothing in module __main__:
do_nothing(not_used)

This function does nothing.

This function uses a pass statement to avoid doing anything.

Parameters:
    not_used - a parameter of any type,
               which is not used.
```

Parameters

Parameters allow you to pass values into a function, which can be used in the function's code block. A parameter is like a variable given to a function when it is called, where the parameter can be different every time you call the function. A function does not have to accept any parameters. For a function that should not accept parameters, you leave the parentheses after the function name empty:

```
def no_params():
    print("I don't listen to nobody")
```

When you call a function, you pass the values for the parameters within the parentheses following the function name. Parameter values can be set based on the position at which they are passed or based on keywords. Functions can be defined to require their parameters be passed in either or a combination of these ways. The values passed to a function are attached to variables with the names defined in the function definition. Listing 6.3 defines three parameters: first, second, and third. These variables are then available to the code block that follows, which prints out the values for each parameter.

Listing 6.3   **Parameters by Position or Keyword**

```
def does_order(first, second, third):
    '''Prints parameters.'''
    print(f'First:  {first}')
    print(f'Second: {second}')
    print(f'Third:  {third}')
```

```
does_order(1, 2, 3)
First:  1
Second: 2
Third:  3

does_order(first=1, second=2, third=3)
First:  1
Second: 2
Third:  3

does_order(1, third=3, second=2)
First:  1
Second: 2
Third:  3
```

Listing 6.3 defines the function does_order() and then calls it three times. The first time, it uses the position of the arguments, (1, 2, 3), to assign the variable values. It assigns the first value to the first parameter, first, the second value to the second parameter, second, and the third value to the third parameter, third.

The second time the listing calls the function does_order(), it uses keyword assignment, explicitly assigning the values using the parameter names, (first=1, second=2, third=3). In the third call, the first parameter is assigned by position, and the other two are assigned using keyword assignment. Notice that in all three cases, the parameters are assigned the same values.

Keyword assignments do not rely on the position of the keywords. For example, you can assign third=3 in the position before second=2 without issue. You cannot use a keyword assignment to the left of a positional assignment, however:

```
does_order(second=2, 1, 3)
File "<ipython-input-9-eed80203e699>", line 1
  does_order(second=2, 1, 3)
                      ^
SyntaxError: positional argument follows keyword argument
```

You can require that a parameter be called only using the keyword method by putting a * to its left in the function definition. All parameters to the right of the star can only be called using keywords. Listing 6.4 shows how to make the parameter third a required keyword parameter and then call it using the keyword syntax.

Listing 6.4 **Parameters Requiring Keywords**

```
def does_keyword(first, second, *, third):
    '''Prints parameters.'''
    print(f'First: {first}')
    print(f'Second: {second}')
    print(f'Third: {third}')
```

```
does_keyword(1, 2, third=3)
First: 1
Second: 2
Third:  3
```

If you try to call a required keyword parameter using positional syntax, you get an error:

```
does_keyword(1, 2, 3)
----------------------------------------------------------------------

    TypeError Traceback (most recent call last)
<ipython-input-15-88b97f8a6c32> in <module>
----> 1 does_keyword(1, 2, 3)


TypeError: does_keyword() takes 2 positional arguments but 3 were given
```

You can make a parameter optional by assigning to it a default value in the function definition. This value will be used if no value is provided for the parameter during the function call. Listing 6.5 defines a function, does_defaults(), whose third parameter has the default value 3. The function is then called twice: first using positional assignment for all three parameters and then using the default value for the third.

Listing 6.5   **Parameters with Defaults**

```
def does_defaults(first, second, third=3):
    '''Prints parameters.'''
    print(f'First:  {first}')
    print(f'Second: {second}')
    print(f'Third:  {third}')

does_defaults(1, 2, 3)
First:  1
Second: 2
Third:  3

does_defaults(1, 2)
First:  1
Second: 2
Third:  3
```

Much as with the restriction regarding the order of keyword and position arguments during a function call, you cannot define a function with a default value parameter to the left of a non-default value parameter:

```
def does_defaults(first=1, second, third=3):
    '''Prints parameters.'''
    print(f'First: {first}')
    print(f'Second: {second}')
    print(f'Third: {third}')
```

```
File "<ipython-input-19-a015eaeb01be>", line 1
    def does_defaults(first=1, second, third=3):
                 ^
SyntaxError: non-default argument follows default argument
```

Default values are defined in the function definition, not in the function call. This means that if you use a mutable object, such as a list or dictionary, as a default value, it will be created once for the function. Every time you call that function using that default, the same list or dictionary object will be used. This can lead to subtle problems if it is not expected. Listing 6.6 defines a function with a list as the default argument. The code block appends 1 to the list. Notice that every time the function is called, the list retains the values from previous calls.

Listing 6.6   **Mutable Defaults**

```
def does_list_default(my_list=[]):
    '''Uses list as default.'''
    my_list.append(1)
    print(my_list)


does_list_default()
[1]


does_list_default()
[1, 1]


does_list_default()
 [1, 1, 1]
```

Generally, it's a good practice to avoid using mutable objects as default parameters to avoid difficult-to-trace bugs and confusion. Listing 6.7 demonstrates a common pattern to handle default values for mutable parameter types. The default value in the function definition is set to None. The code block tests whether the parameter has an assigned value. If it does not, a new list is created and assigned to the variable. Because the list is created in the code block, a new list is created every time the function is called without a value supplied for the parameter.

Listing 6.7   **Default Pattern in a Code Block**

```
def does_list_param(my_list=None):
    '''Assigns default in code to avoid confusion.'''
    my_list = my_list or []
    my_list.append(1)
    print(my_list)


does_list_param()
[1]
```

```
does_list_param()
[1]

does_list_param()
[1]
```

As of Python 3.8, you can restrict parameters to positional assignment only. A parameter to the left of a forward slash (/) in a function definition is restricted to positional assignment. Listing 6.8 defines the function does_positional so that its first parameter, first, is positional only.

Listing 6.8   **Positional-Only Parameters (Python 3.8 and Later)**

```
def does_positional(first, /, second, third):
    '''Demonstrates a positional parameter.'''
    print(f'First:  {first}')
    print(f'Second: {second}')
    print(f'Third:  {third}')

does_positional(1, 2, 3)
First:  1
Second: 2
Third:  3
```

If you try to call does_positional by using keyword assignment for first, you get an error:

```
does_positional(first=1, second=2, third=3)
-------------------------------------------------------------------------
TypeError Traceback (most recent call las t)
<ipython-input-24-7b1f45f64358> in <module>
----> 1 does_positional(first=1, second=2, third=3)
TypeError: does_positional() got some positional-only arguments passed as
keyword arguments: 'first'
```

Listing 6.9 modifies does_positional to use positional-only and keyword-only parameters. The parameter first is positional only, the parameter second can be set using positional or keyword assignment, and the last, third, is keyword only.

Listing 6.9   **Positional-Only and Keyword-Only Parameters**

```
def does_positional(first, /, second, *, third):
    '''Demonstrates a positional and keyword parameters.'''
    print(f'First:  {first}')
    print(f'Second: {second}')
    print(f'Third:  {third}')

does_positional(1, 2, third=3)
First:  1
Second: 2
Third:  3
```

You can use wildcards in function definitions to accept an undefined number of positional or keyword arguments. This is often done when a function calls a function from an outside API. The function can pass the arguments through without requiring that all of the outside API's parameters be defined.

To use a wildcard for positional parameters, you use the * character. Listing 6.10 demonstrates the definition of a function with the positional wildcard parameter *args. The code block receives any positional arguments given in a function call as items in a list named args. This function goes through the list and prints each item. The function is then called with the arguments 'Donkey', 3, and ['a'], each of which is accessed from the list and printed.

Listing 6.10   **Positional Wildcard Parameters**

```
def does_wildcard_positions(*args):
    '''Demonstrates wildcard for positional parameters.'''
    for item in args:
        print(item)

does_wildcard_positions('Donkey', 3, ['a'])
Donkey
3
['a']
```

To define a function with keyword wildcard parameters, you define a parameter that starts with **. For example, Listing 6.11 defines the function does_wildcard_keywords with the parameter **kwargs. In the code block, the keyword parameters are available as keys and values in the dictionary kwargs.

Listing 6.11   **Keyword Wildcard Parameters**

```
def does_wildcard_keywords(**kwargs):
    '''Demonstrates wildcard for keyword parameters.'''
    for key, value in kwargs.items():
        print(f'{key} : {value}')

does_wildcard_keywords(one=1, name='Martha')
one : 1
name : Martha
```

You can use both positional and keyword wildcard parameters in the same function: Just define the positional parameters first and the keyword parameters second. Listing 6.12 demonstrates a function using both positional and keyword parameters.

Listing 6.12   **Positional and Keyword Wildcard Parameters**

```
def does_wildcards(*args, **kwargs):
    '''Demonstrates wildcard parameters.'''
    print(f'Positional: {args}')
    print(f'Keyword: {kwargs}')
```

```
does_wildcards(1, 2, a='a', b=3)
Positional: (1, 2)
Keyword: {'a': 'a', 'b': 3}
```

Return Statements

Return statements define what value a function evaluates to when called. A return statement consists of the keyword `return` followed by an expression. The expression can be a simple value, a more complicated calculation, or a call to another function. Listing 6.13 defines a function that takes a number as an argument and returns that number plus 1.

Listing 6.13   **Return Value**

```
def adds_one(some_number):
    '''Demonstrates return statement.'''
    return some_number + 1

adds_one(1)
2
```

Every Python function has a return value. If you do not define a return statement explicitly, the function returns the special value None:

```
def returns_none():
    '''Demonstrates default return value.'''
    pass

returns_none() == None
True
```

This example omits a return statement and then tests that the value returned is equal to None.

Scope in Functions

Scope refers to the availability of objects defined in code. A variable defined in the global scope is available throughout your code, whereas a variable defined in a local scope is available only in that scope. Listing 6.14 defines a variable `outer` and a variable `inner`. Both variables are available in the code block of the function `shows_scope`, where you print them both.

Listing 6.14   **Local and Global Scope**

```
outer = 'Global scope'

def shows_scope():
    '''Demonstrates local variable.'''
    inner = 'Local scope'
    print(outer)
    print(inner)
```

```
shows_scope()
Global scope
Local scope
```

The variable inner is local to the function, as it is defined in the function's code block. If you try to call inner from outside the function, it is not defined:

```
print(inner)
---------------------------------------------------------------------
NameError Traceback (most recent call last)
<ipython-input-39-9504624e1153> in <module>
----> 1 print(inner)
NameError: name 'inner' is not defined
```

Understanding scope is useful when you use decorators, as described in the next section.

Decorators

A decorator enables you to design functions that modify other functions. Decorators are commonly used to set up logging using a set convention or by third-party libraries. While you may not need to write your own decorators, it is useful to understand how they work. This section walks through the concepts involved.

In Python, everything is an object, including functions. This means you can point a variable to a function. Listing 6.15 defines the function add_one(n), which takes a number and adds 1 to it. Next, it creates the variable my_func, which has the function add_one() as its value.

> **Note**
>
> When you are not calling a function, you do not use parentheses in the variable assignment. By omitting the parentheses, you are referring to the function object and not to a return value. You can see this where Listing 6.15 prints my_func, which is indeed a function object. You can then call the function by adding the parentheses and argument to my_func, which returns the argument plus 1.

Listing 6.15   **A Function as Variable Value**

```
def add_one(n):
    '''Adds one to a number.'''
    return n + 1

my_func = add_one
print(my_func)
<function add_one at 0x1075953a0>

my_func(2)
3
```

Because functions are objects, you can use them with data structures such as dictionaries or lists. Listing 6.16 defines two functions and puts them in a list pointed to by the variable my_functions. It then iterates through the list, assigning each function to the variable my_func during its iteration and calling the function during the for loop's code block.

Listing 6.16   **Calling a List of Functions**

```
def add_one(n):
    '''Adds one to a number.'''
    return n + 1

def add_two(n):
    '''Adds two to a number.'''
    return n + 2

my_functions = [add_one, add_two]

for my_func in my_functions:
    print(my_func(1))
2
3
```

Python allows you to define a function as part of another function's code block. A function defined in this way is called a *nested function*. Listing 6.17 defines the function nested() in the code block of the function called_nested(). This nested function is then used as a return value for the outer function.

Listing 6.17   **Nested Functions**

```
def call_nested():
    '''Calls a nested function.'''
    print('outer')

    def nested():
        '''Prints a message.'''
        print('nested')

    return nested

my_func = call_nested()
outer
my_func()
nested
```

You can also wrap one function with another, adding functionality before or after. Listing 6.18 wraps the function add_one(number) with the function wrapper(number). The wrapping function takes a parameter, number, which it then passes to the wrapped function. It also has

statements before and after calling add_one(number). You can see the order of the print
statements when you call wrapper(1) and see that it returns the expected values from
add_one: 1 and 2.

Listing 6.18   **Wrapping Functions**

```
def add_one(number):
    '''Adds to a number.'''
    print('Adding 1')
    return number + 1

def wrapper(number):
    '''Wraps another function.'''
    print('Before calling function')
    retval = add_one(number)
    print('After calling function')
    return retval

wrapper(1)
Before calling function
Adding 1
After calling function
2
```

It is also possible to go a step further and use a function as a parameter. You can pass a function
as a value to a function that has a nested function definition wrapping the function that was
passed. For example, Listing 6.19 first defines the function add_one(number) as before. But
now it defines the function wrapper(number) nested in the code block of a new function,
do_wrapping(some_func). This new function takes a function as an argument and then uses
that function in the definition of wrapper(number). It then returns the newly defined version of
wrapper(number). By assigning this result to a variable and calling it, you can see the wrapped
results.

Listing 6.19   **Nested Wrapping Function**

```
def add_one(number):
    '''Adds to a number.'''
    print('Adding 1')
    return number + 1

def do_wrapping(some_func):
    '''Returns a wrapped function.'''
    print('wrapping function')

    def wrapper(number):
        '''Wraps another function.'''
        print('Before calling function')
        retval = some_func(number)
```

```
        print('After calling function')
        return retval

    return wrapper

my_func = do_wrapping(add_one)
wrapping function

my_func(1)
Before calling function
Adding 1
After calling function
2
```

You can use do_wrapping(some_func) to wrap any function that you like. For example, if you have the function add_two(number), you can pass it as an argument just as you did add_one(number):

```
my_func = do_wrapping(add_two)
my_func(1)
wrapping function
Before calling function
Adding 2
After calling function
3
```

Decorators provide syntax that can simplify this type of function wrapping. Instead of calling do_wrapping(some_func), assigning it to a variable, and then invoking the function from the variable, you can simply put @do_wrapping at the top of the function definition. Then the function add_one(number) can be called directly, and the wrapping happens behind the scenes.

You can see in Listing 6.20 that add_one(number) is wrapped in a similar fashion as in Listing 6.18, but with the simpler decorator syntax.

Listing 6.20 **Decorator Syntax**

```
def do_wrapping(some_func):
    '''Returns a wrapped function.'''
    print('wrapping function')

    def wrapper(number):
        '''Wraps another function.'''
        print('Before calling function')
        retval = some_func(number)
        print('After calling function')
        return retval

    return wrapper
```

```
@do_wrapping
def add_one(number):
    '''Adds to a number.'''
    print('Adding 1')
    return number + 1
wrapping function

add_one(1)
Before calling function
Adding 1
After calling function
2
```

Anonymous Functions

The vast majority of the time you define functions, you will want to use the syntax for named functions. This is what you have seen up to this point. There is an alternative, however: the unnamed, anonymous function. In Python, anonymous functions are known as lambda functions, and they have the following syntax:

```
lambda <Parameter>: <Statement>
```

where lambda is the keyword designating a lambda function, <Parameter> is an input parameter, and <Statement> is the statement to execute using the parameter. The result of <Statement> is the return value. This is how you define a lambda function that adds one to an input value:

```
lambda x: x +1
```

In general, your code will be easier to read, use, and debug if you avoid lambda functions, but one useful place for them is when a simple function is applied as an argument to another. Listing 6.21 defines the function apply_to_list(data, my_func), which takes a list and a function as arguments. When you call this function with the intention of adding 1 to each member of the list, the lambda function is an elegant solution.

Listing 6.21 **Lambda Function**

```
def apply_to_list(data, my_func):
    '''Applies a function to items in a list.'''
    for item in data:
        print(f'{my_func(item)}')

apply_to_list([1, 2, 3], lambda x: x + 1)
2
3
4
```

Summary

Functions, which are important building blocks in constructing complex programs, are reusable named blocks of code. Functions are documented with docstrings. Functions can accept parameters in a number of ways. A function uses a return statement to pass a value at the end of its execution. Decorators are special functions that wrap other functions. Anonymous, or lambda, functions are unnamed.

Questions

For Questions 1–3, refer to Listing 6.22.

Listing 6.22   **Functions for Questions 1–3**

```
def add_prefix(word, prefix='before-'):
    '''Prepend a word.'''
    return f'{prefix}{word}'3

def return_one():
    return 1

    def wrapper():
        print('a')
        retval = return_one()
        print('b')
        print(retval)
```

1. What would be the output of the following call:

   `add_prefix('nighttime', 'after-')`

2. What would be the output of the following call:

   `add_prefix('nighttime')`

3. What would be the output of the following call:

   `add_prefix()`

4. Which line should you put above a function definition to decorate it with the function standard_logging?

   ```
   *standard_logging
   **standard_logging
   @standard_logging
   [standard_logging]
   ```

5. What would be printed by the following call:

   `wrapper()`

Part II
Data Science Libraries

NumPy

Everything should be as simple as it can be, but not simpler.

Roger Sessions (interpreting Einstein)

In This Chapter

- Introducing third-party libraries
- Creating NumPy arrays
- Indexing and slicing arrays
- Filtering array data
- Array methods
- Broadcasting

This is the first of this book's chapters on Data Science Libraries. The Python functionality explored so far in this book makes Python a powerful generic language. The libraries covered in this part of the book make Python dominant in data science. The first library we will look at, NumPy, is the backbone of many of the other data science libraries. In this chapter, you will learn about the NumPy array, which is an efficient multidimensional data structure.

Third-Party Libraries

Python code is organized into libraries. All of the functionality you have seen so far in this book is available in the Python Standard Library, which is part of any Python installation. Third-party libraries give you capabilities far beyond this. They are developed and maintained by groups outside the organization that maintains Python itself. The existence of these groups and libraries creates a vibrant ecosystem that has kept Python a dominant player in the programming world. Many of these libraries are available in the Colab environment, and you can easily import them into a file. If you are working outside Colab, you may need to install them, which generally is done using the Python package manager, `pip`.

Installing and Importing NumPy

NumPy is preinstalled in the Colab environment, and you just need to import it. If you are working outside Colab, there are a few different ways to install it (enumerated at https://scipy.org/install.html), but the most common is to use pip:

```
pip install numpy
```

Once you have NumPy installed, you can import it. When you import any library, you can change what it is called in your environment by using the keyword as. NumPy is typically renamed np during import:

```
import numpy as np
```

When you have the library installed and imported, you can then access any of NumPy's functionality through the np object.

Creating Arrays

A NumPy array is a data structure that is designed to efficiently handle operations on large data sets. These data sets can be of varying dimensions and can contain numerous data types—though not in the same object. NumPy arrays are used as input and output to many other libraries and are used as the underpinning of other data structures that are important to data science, such as those in Pandas and SciPy.

You can create arrays from other data structures or initialized with set values. Listing 7.1 demonstrates different ways to create a one-dimensional array. You can see that the array object is displayed as having an internal list as its data. Data is not actually stored in lists, but this representation makes arrays easy to read.

Listing 7.1 **Creating an Array**

```
np.array([1,2,3])      # Array from list
array([1, 2, 3])

np.zeros(3)            # Array of zeros
array([0., 0., 0.])

np.ones(3)             # Array of ones
array([1., 1., 1.])

np.empty(3)            # Array of arbitrary data
array([1., 1., 1.])

np.arange(3)           # Array from range of numbers
array([0, 1, 2])
```

```
np.arange(0, 12, 3)     # Array from range of numbers
array([0, 3, 6, 9])

np.linspace(0, 21, 7)  # Array over an interval
array([ 0. ,   3.5,  7. , 10.5, 14. , 17.5, 21. ])
```

Arrays have dimensions. A one-dimensional array has only one dimension, which is the number of elements. In the case of the np.array method, the dimension matches that of the list(s) used as input. For the np.zeros, np.ones, and np.empty methods, the dimension is given as an explicit argument.

The np.range method produces an array in a way similar to a range sequence. The resulting dimension and values match those that would be produced by using range. You can specify beginning, ending, and step values.

The np.linspace method produces evenly spaced numbers over an interval. The first two arguments define the interval, and the third defines the number of items.

The np.empty method is useful in producing large arrays efficiently. Keep in mind that because the data is arbitrary, you should only use it in cases where you will replace all of the original data.

Listing 7.2 shows some of the attributes of an array.

Listing 7.2   **Characteristics of an Array**

```
oned = np.arange(21)
oned
array([ 0,  1,  2,  3,  4,  5,  6,  7,  8,  9, 10,
       11, 12, 13, 14, 15, 16, 17, 18, 19, 20 ])

oned.dtype      # Data type
dtype('int64')

oned.size       # Number of elements
21

oned.nbytes     # Bytes(memory) consumed by elements of the array
168

oned.shape      # Number of elements in each dimension
(21,)

oned.ndim       # Number of dimensions
1
```

If you check the data type of the array, you see that it is np.ndarray:

```
type(oned)
numpy.ndarray
```

> **Note**
>
> ndarray is short for *n-dimensional array*.

As mentioned earlier, you can make arrays of many dimensions. Two-dimensional arrays are used as matrixes. Listing 7.3 creates a two-dimensional array from a list of three three-element lists. You can see that the resulting array has 3×3 shape and two dimensions.

Listing 7.3 **Matrix from Lists**

```
list_o_lists = [[1,2,3],
                [4,5,6],
                [7,8,9]]

twod = np.array(list_o_lists)
twod
array([[1, 2, 3],
       [4, 5, 6],
       [7, 8, 9]])

twod.shape
(3, 3)

twod.ndim
2
```

You can produce an array with the same elements but different dimensions by using the reshape method. This method takes the new shape as arguments. Listing 7.4 demonstrates using a one-dimensional array to produce a two-dimensional one and then producing one-dimensional and three-dimensional arrays from the two-dimensional one.

Listing 7.4 **Using reshape**

```
oned = np.arange(12)
oned
array([ 0,  1,  2,  3,  4,  5,  6,  7,  8,  9, 10, 11])

twod = oned.reshape(3,4)
twod
array([[ 0,  1,  2,  3],
       [ 4,  5,  6,  7],
       [ 8,  9, 10, 11]])

twod.reshape(12)
array([ 0,  1,  2,  3,  4,  5,  6,  7,  8,  9, 10, 11])
```

```
twod.reshape(2,2,3)
array([[[ 0,  1,  2],
        [ 3,  4,  5]],
       [[ 6,  7,  8],
        [ 9, 10, 11]]])
```

The shape you provide for an array must be consistent with the number of elements in it. For example, if you take the 12-element array twod and try to set its dimensions with a shape that does not include 12 elements, you get an error:

```
twod.reshape(2,3)
-------------------------------------------------------------------
ValueError                          Traceback (most recent call last)
<ipython-input-295-0b0517f762ed> in <module>
----> 1 twod.reshape(2,3)

ValueError: cannot reshape array of size 12 into shape (2,3)
```

Reshaping is commonly used with the np.zeros, np.ones, and np.empty methods to produce multidimensional arrays with default values. For example, you could create a three-dimensional array of ones like this:

```
np.ones(12).reshape(2,3,2)
array([[[1., 1.],
        [1., 1.],
        [1., 1.]],
       [[1., 1.],
        [1., 1.],
        [1., 1.]]])
```

Indexing and Slicing

You can access the data in arrays by indexing and slicing. In Listing 7.5, you can see that indexing and slicing with a one-dimensional array is the same as with a list. You can index individual elements from the start or end of an array by supplying an index number or multiple elements using a slice.

Listing 7.5   **Indexing and Slicing a one-Dimensional Array**

```
oned = np.arange(21)
oned
array([ 0,  1,  2,  3,  4,  5,  6,  7,  8,  9, 10,
       11, 12, 13, 14, 15, 16, 17, 18, 19, 20 ])

oned[3]
3
```

```
oned[-1]
20
```

```
oned[3:9]
array([3, 4, 5, 6, 7, 8])
```

For multidimensional arrays, you can supply one argument for each dimension. If you omit the argument for a dimension, it defaults to all elements of that dimension. So, if you supply a single number as an argument to a two-dimensional array, that number will indicate which row to return. If you supply single-number arguments for all dimensions, a single element is returned. You can also supply a slice for any dimension. In return you get a subarray of elements, whose dimensions are determined by the length of your slices. Listing 7.6 demonstrates various options for indexing and slicing a two-dimensional array.

Listing 7.6   Indexing and Slicing a Two-Dimensional Array

```
twod = np.arange(21).reshape(3,7)
twod
array([[ 0,  1,  2,  3,  4,  5,  6],
       [ 7,  8,  9, 10, 11, 12, 13],
       [14, 15, 16, 17, 18, 19, 20]])
```

```
twod[2]            # Accessing row 2
array([14, 15, 16, 17, 18, 19, 20])
```

```
twod[2, 3]         # Accessing item at row 2, column 3
17
```

```
twod[0:2]          # Accessing rows 0 and 1
array([[ 0,  1,  2,  3,  4,  5,  6],
       [ 7,  8,  9, 10, 11, 12, 13]])
```

```
twod[:, 3]         # Accessing column 3 of all rows
array([ 3, 10, 17])
```

```
twod[0:2, -3:]     # Accessing the last three columns of rows 0 and 1
array([[ 4,  5,  6],
       [11, 12, 13]])
```

You can assign new values to an existing array, much as you would with a list, by using indexing and slicing. If you assign a values to a slice, the whole slice is updated with the new value. Listing 7.7 demonstrates how to update a single element and a slice of a two-dimensional array.

Listing 7.7   **Changing Values in an Array**

```
twod = np.arange(21).reshape(3,7)
twod
array([[ 0,  1,  2,  3,  4,  5,  6],
       [ 7,  8,  9, 10, 11, 12, 13],
       [14, 15, 16, 17, 18, 19, 20]])

twod[0,0] = 33
twod
array([[33,  1,  2,  3,  4,  5,  6],
       [ 7,  8,  9, 10, 11, 12, 13],
       [14, 15, 16, 17, 18, 19, 20]])

twod[1:,:3] = 0
array([[33,  1,  2,  3,  4,  5,  6],
       [ 0,  0,  0, 10, 11, 12, 13],
       [ 0,  0,  0, 17, 18, 19, 20]])
```

Element-by-Element Operations

An array is not a sequence. Arrays do share some characteristics with lists, and on some level it is easy to think of the data in an array as a list of lists. There are many differences between arrays and sequences, however. One area of difference is when performing operations between the items in two arrays or two sequences.

Remember that when you do an operation such as multiplication with a sequence, the operation is done to the sequence, not to its contents. So, if you multiply a list by zero, the result is a list with a length of zero:

```
[1, 2, 3]*0
[]
```

You cannot multiply two lists, even if they are the same length:

```
[1, 2, 3]*[4, 5, 6]
--------------------------------------------------------------------------
TypeError                                Traceback (most recent call last)
<ipython-input-325-f525a1e96937> in <module>
----> 1 [1, 2, 3]*[4, 5, 6]

TypeError: can't multiply sequence by non-int of type 'list'
```

You can write code to perform operations between the elements of lists. For example, Listing 7.8 demonstrates looping through two lists in order to create a third list that contains the results of multiple pairs of elements. The zip() function is used to combine the two lists into a list of tuples, with each tuple containing elements from each of the original lists.

Listing 7.8   **Element-by-Element Operations with Lists**

```
L1 = list(range(10))
L2 = list(range(10, 0, -1))
L1
[0, 1, 2, 3, 4, 5, 6, 7, 8, 9]

L2
 [10, 9, 8, 7, 6, 5, 4, 3, 2, 1]

L3 = []
for i, j in zip(L1, L2):
L3.append(i*j)
L3
[0, 9, 16, 21, 24, 25, 24, 21, 16, 9]
```

While it is possible to use loops to perform element-by-element operations on lists, it is much simpler to use NumPy arrays for such operations. Arrays do element-by-element operations by default. Listing 7.9 demonstrates multiplication, addition, and division operations between two arrays. Notice that the operations in each case are done between the elements of the arrays.

Listing 7.9   **Element-by-Element Operations with Arrays**

```
array1 = np.array(L1)
array2 = np.array(L2)
array1*array2
array([ 0,  9, 16, 21, 24, 25, 24, 21, 16,  9])

array1 + array2
array([10, 10, 10, 10, 10, 10, 10, 10, 10, 10])

array1 / array2
array([0.        , 0.11111111, 0.25      , 0.42857143, 0.66666667,
       1.        , 1.5       , 2.33333333, 4.        , 9.        ])
```

Filtering Values

One of the most used aspects of NumPy arrays and the data structures built on top of them is the ability to filter values based on conditions of your choosing. In this way, you can use an array to answer questions about your data.

Listing 7.10 shows a two-dimensional array of integers, called twod. A second array, mask, has the same dimensions as twod, but it contains Boolean values. mask specifies which elements from twod to return. The resulting array contains the elements from twod whose corresponding positions in mask have the value True.

Listing 7.10   **Filtering Using Booleans**

```
twod = np.arange(21).reshape(3,7)
twod
array([[ 0,  1,  2,  3,  4,  5,  6],
       [ 7,  8,  9, 10, 11, 12, 13],
       [14, 15, 16, 17, 18, 19, 20]])

mask = np.array([[ True,  False,  True,  True,  False, True, False],
                 [ True,  False,  True,  True,  False, True, False],
                 [ True,  False,  True,  True,  False, True, False]])
twod[mask]
array([ 0,  2,  3,  5,  7,  9, 10, 12, 14, 16, 17, 19])
```

Comparison operators that you have seen returning single Booleans before return arrays when used with arrays. So, if you use the less-than operator (<) against the array twod as follows, the result will be an array with True for every item that is below five and False for the rest:

```
twod < 5
```

You can use this result as a mask to get only the values that are True with the comparison. For example, Listing 7.11 creates a mask and then returns only the values of twod that are less than 5.

Listing 7.11   **Filtering Using Comparison**

```
mask = twod < 5
mask
array([[ True,  True,  True,  True],
       [ True, False, False, False],
       [False, False, False, False]])

twod[mask]
array([0, 1, 2, 3, 4])
```

As you can see, you can use comparison and order operators to easily extract knowledge from data. You can also combine these comparisons to create more complex masks. Listing 7.12 uses & to join two conditions to create a mask that evaluates to True only for items meeting both conditions.

Listing 7.12   **Filtering Using Multiple Comparisons**

```
mask = (twod < 5) & (twod%2 == 0)
mask
array([[ True, False,  True, False],
       [ True, False, False, False],
       [False, False, False, False]])

twod[mask]
array([0, 2, 4])
```

> **Note**
>
> Filtering using masks is a process that you will use time and time again, especially with Pandas DataFrames, which are built on top of NumPy arrays. You will learn about DataFrames in Chapter 9, "Pandas."

Views Versus Copies

NumPy arrays are designed to work efficiently with large data sets. One of the ways this is accomplished is by using views. When you slice or filter an array, the returned array is, when possible, a view and not a copy. A view allows you to look at the same data differently. It is important to understand that memory and processing power are not used in making copies of data every time you slice or filter. If you change a value in a view of an array, you change that value in the original array as well as any other views that represent that item. For example, Listing 7.13 takes a slice from the array data1 and names it data2. It then replace the value 11 in data2 with -1. When you go back to data1, you can see that the item that used to have a value of 11 is now set to -1.

Listing 7.13   **Changing Values in a View**

```
data1 = np.arange(24).reshape(4,6)
data1
array([[ 0,  1,  2,  3,  4,  5],
       [ 6,  7,  8,  9, 10, 11],
       [12, 13, 14, 15, 16, 17],
       [18, 19, 20, 21, 22, 23]])

data2 = data1[:2,3:]
data2
array([[ 3,  4,  5],
       [ 9, 10, 11]])

data2[1,2] = -1
data2
array([[ 3,  4,  5],
       [ 9, 10, -1]])

data1
array([[ 0,  1,  2,  3,  4,  5],
       [ 6,  7,  8,  9, 10, -1],
       [12, 13, 14, 15, 16, 17],
       [18, 19, 20, 21, 22, 23]])
```

This behavior can lead to bugs and miscalculations, but if you understand it, you can gain some important benefits when working with large data sets. If you want to change data from a slice or filtering operation without changing it in the original array, you can make a copy. For example, in Listing 7.14, notice that when an item is changed in the copy, the original array remains unchanged.

Listing 7.14   **Changing Values in a Copy**

```
data1 = np.arange(24).reshape(4,6)
data1
array([[ 0,  1,  2,  3,  4,  5],
       [ 6,  7,  8,  9, 10, 11],
       [12, 13, 14, 15, 16, 17],
       [18, 19, 20, 21, 22, 23]])

data2 = data1[:2,3:].copy()
data2
array([[ 3,  4,  5],
       [ 9, 10, 11]])

data2[1,2] = -1
data2
array([[ 3,  4,  5],
       [ 9, 10, -1]])

data1
array([[ 0,  1,  2,  3,  4,  5],
       [ 6,  7,  8,  9, 10, 11],
       [12, 13, 14, 15, 16, 17],
       [18, 19, 20, 21, 22, 23]])
```

Some Array Methods

NumPy arrays have built-in methods both to get statistical summary data and to perform matrix operations. Listing 7.15 shows methods producing summary statistics. There are methods to get the maximum, minimum, sum, mean, and standard deviation. All these methods produce results across the whole array unless an axis is specified. If an axis value of 1 is specified, an array with results for each row is produced. With an axis value of 0, an array of results is produced for each column.

Listing 7.15   **Introspection**

```
data = np.arange(12).reshape(3,4)
data
array([[ 0,  1,  2,  3],
       [ 4,  5,  6,  7],
       [ 8,  9, 10, 11]])

data.max()        # Maximum value
11

data.min()        # Minimum value
0
```

```
data.sum()          # Sum of all values
66

data.mean()         # Mean of values
5.5

data.std()          # Standard deviation
3.452052529534663

data.sum(axis=1)    # Sum of each row
array([ 6, 22, 38])

data.sum(axis=0)    # Sum of each column
array([12, 15, 18, 21])

data.std(axis=0)    # Standard deviation of each row
array([3.26598632, 3.26598632, 3.26598632, 3.26598632])

data.std(axis=1))   # Standard deviation of each column
array([1.11803399, 1.11803399, 1.11803399])
```

Listing 7.16 demonstrates some of the matrix operations that are available with arrays. These include returning the transpose, returning matrix products, and returning the diagonal. Remember that you can use the multiplication operator (*) between arrays to perform element-by-element multiplication. If you want to calculate the dot product of two matrices, you need to use the @ operator or the .dot() method.

Listing 7.16 **Matrix Operations**

```
A1 = np.arange(9).reshape(3,3)
A1
array([[0, 1, 2],
       [3, 4, 5],
       [6, 7, 8]])

A1.T              # Transpose
array([[0, 3, 6],
       [1, 4, 7],
       [2, 5, 8]])


A2 = np.ones(9).reshape(3,3)
array([[1., 1., 1.],
       [1., 1., 1.],
       [1., 1., 1.]])
```

```
A1 @ A2           # Matrix product
array([[ 3.,   3.,   3.],
       [12., 12., 12.],
       [21., 21., 21.]])

A1.dot(A2)        # Dot product
array([[ 3.,   3.,   3.],
       [12., 12., 12.],
       [21., 21., 21.]])

A1.diagonal()     # Diagonal
array([0, 4, 8])
```

An array, unlike many sequence types, can contain only one data type. You cannot have an array that contains both strings and integers. If you do not specify the data type, NumPy guesses the type, based on the data. Listing 7.17 shows that when you start with integers, NumPy sets the data type to int64. You can also see, by checking the nbytes attribute, that the data for this array takes 800 bytes of memory.

Listing 7.17   **Setting Type Automatically**

```
darray = np.arange(100)
darray
array([ 0,  1,  2,  3,  4,  5,  6,  7,  8,  9, 10, 11, 12, 13, 14, 15, 16,
       17, 18, 19, 20, 21, 22, 23, 24, 25, 26, 27, 28, 29, 30, 31, 32, 33,
       34, 35, 36, 37, 38, 39, 40, 41, 42, 43, 44, 45, 46, 47, 48, 49, 50,
       51, 52, 53, 54, 55, 56, 57, 58, 59, 60, 61, 62, 63, 64, 65, 66, 67,
       68, 69, 70, 71, 72, 73, 74, 75, 76, 77, 78, 79, 80, 81, 82, 83, 84,
       85, 86, 87, 88, 89, 90, 91, 92, 93, 94, 95, 96, 97, 98, 99])

darray.dtype
dtype('int64')

darray.nbytes
800
```

For lager data sets, you can control the amount of memory used by setting the data type explicitly. The int8 data type can represent numbers from –128 to 127, so it would be adequate for a data set of 1–99. You can set an array's data type at creation by using the parameter dtype. Listing 7.18 does this to bring the size of the data down to 100 bytes.

Listing 7.18   **Setting Type Explicitly**

```
darray = np.arange(100, dtype=np.int8)
darray
array([ 0,  1,  2,  3,  4,  5,  6,  7,  8,  9, 10, 11, 12, 13, 14, 15, 16,
       17, 18, 19, 20, 21, 22, 23, 24, 25, 26, 27, 28, 29, 30, 31, 32, 33,
```

```
       34, 35, 36, 37, 38, 39, 40, 41, 42, 43, 44, 45, 46, 47, 48, 49, 50,
       51, 52, 53, 54, 55, 56, 57, 58, 59, 60, 61, 62, 63, 64, 65, 66, 67,
       68, 69, 70, 71, 72, 73, 74, 75, 76, 77, 78, 79, 80, 81, 82, 83, 84,
       85, 86, 87, 88, 89, 90, 91, 92, 93, 94, 95, 96, 97, 98, 99],
       dtype=int8)
```

darray.nbytes
100

> **Note**
>
> You can see the many available NumPy data types at https://numpy.org/devdocs/user/
> basics.types.html.

Because an array can store only one data type, you cannot insert data that cannot be cast to that
data type. For example, if you try to add a string to the int8 array, you get an error:

darray[14] = 'a'
```
--------------------------------------------------------------------------
ValueError                            Traceback (most recent call last)
<ipython-input-335-17df5782f85b> in <module>
----> 1 darray[14] = 'a'


ValueError: invalid literal for int() with base 10: 'a'
```

A subtle error with array type occurs if you add to an array data of a finer granularity than the
array's data type; this can lead to data loss. For example, say that you add the floating-point
number 0.5 to the int8 array:

darray[14] = 0.5

The floating-point number 0.5 is cast to an int, which leaves a value of 0:

darray[14]
0

As you can see, it is important to understand your data when deciding on the best data type.

Broadcasting

You can perform operations between arrays of different dimensions. Operations can be done
when the dimension is the same or when the dimension is one for at least one of the arrays.
Listing 7.19 adds 1 to each element of the array A1 three different ways: first with an array of ones
with the same dimensions (3, 3), then with an array with one dimension of one (1, 3), and finally
by using the integer 1.

Listing 7.19   **Broadcasting**

```
A1 = np.array([[1,2,3],
               [4,5,6],
               [7,8,9]])
```

```
A2 = np.array([[1,1,1],
               [1,1,1],
               [1,1,1]])

A1 + A2
array([[ 2,  3,  4],
       [ 5,  6,  7],
       [ 8,  9, 10]])

A2 = np.array([1,1,1])
A1 + A2
array([[ 2,  3,  4],
       [ 5,  6,  7],
       [ 8,  9, 10]])

A1 + 1
array([[ 2,  3,  4],
       [ 5,  6,  7],
       [ 8,  9, 10]])
```

In all three cases, the result is the same: an array of dimension (3, 3). This is called *broadcasting* because a dimension of one is expanded to fit the higher dimension. So if you do an operation with arrays of dimensions (1, 3, 4, 4) and (5, 3, 4, 1), the resulting array will have the dimensions (5, 3, 4, 4). Broadcasting does not work with dimensions that are different but not one.

Listing 7.20 does an operation on arrays with the dimensions (2, 1, 5) and (2, 7, 1). The resulting array has the dimensions (2, 7, 5).

Listing 7.20   **Expanding Dimensions**

```
A4 = np.arange(10).reshape(2,1,5)
A4
array([[[0, 1, 2, 3, 4]],
       [[5, 6, 7, 8, 9]]])

A5 = np.arange(14).reshape(2,7,1)
A5
array([[[ 0],
        [ 1],
        [ 2],
        [ 3],
        [ 4],
        [ 5],
        [ 6]],
       [[ 7],
        [ 8],
        [ 9],
        [10],
```

```
                [11],
                [12],
                [13]]])

A6 = A4 - A5
A6
array([[[ 0,  1,  2,  3,  4],
        [-1,  0,  1,  2,  3],
        [-2, -1,  0,  1,  2],
        [-3, -2, -1,  0,  1],
        [-4, -3, -2, -1,  0],
        [-5, -4, -3, -2, -1],
        [-6, -5, -4, -3, -2]],

       [[-2, -1,  0,  1,  2],
        [-3, -2, -1,  0,  1],
        [-4, -3, -2, -1,  0],
        [-5, -4, -3, -2, -1],
        [-6, -5, -4, -3, -2],
        [-7, -6, -5, -4, -3],
        [-8, -7, -6, -5, -4]]])
A6.shape
(2, 7, 5)
```

NumPy Math

In addition to the NumPy array, the NumPy library offers many mathematical functions, including trigonometric functions, logarithmic functions, and arithmetic functions. These functions are designed to be performed with NumPy arrays and are often used in conjunction with data types in other libraries. This section takes a quick look at NumPy polynomials.

NumPy offers the class poly1d for modeling one-dimensional polynomials. To use this class, you need to import it from NumPy:

```
[1]    1 from numpy import poly1d
```

Then create a polynomial object, giving the coefficients as an argument:

```
poly1d((4,5))
poly1d([4, 5])
```

If you print a poly1d object, it shows the polynomial representation:

```
c = poly1d([4,3,2,1])
print(c)
   3     2
4 x + 3 x + 2 x + 1
```

If for a second argument you supply the value True, the first argument is interpreted as roots rather than coefficients. The following example models the polynomial resulting from the calculation (x – 4)(x – 3)(x – 2)(x – 1):

```
r = poly1d([4,3,2,1], True)
print(r)
   4      3      2
1 x - 10 x + 35 x - 50 x + 24
```

You can evaluate a polynomial by supplying the x value as an argument to the object itself. For example, you can evaluate the preceding polynomial for a value of x equal to 5:

```
r(5)
24.0
```

The poly1d class allows you to do operations between polynomials, such as addition and multiplication. It also offers polynomial functionality as special class methods. Listing 7.21 demonstrates the use of this class with polynomials.

Listing 7.21   **Polynomials**

```
p1 = poly1d((2,3))
print(p1)
2 x + 3

p2 = poly1d((1,2,3))
print(p2)
   2
1 x + 2 x + 3

print(p2*p1)          # Multiplying polynomials
   3     2
2 x + 7 x + 12 x + 9

print(p2.deriv())     # Taking the derivative
2 x + 2

print(p2.integ())     # Returning anti-derivative
      3     2
0.3333 x + 1 x + 3 x
```

The poly1d class is just one of the many specialized mathematical tools offered in the NumPy toolkit. These tools are used in conjunction with many of the other specialized tools that you will learn about in the coming chapters.

Summary

The third-party library NumPy is a workhorse for doing data science in Python. Even if you don't use NumPy arrays directly, you will encounter them because they are building blocks for many other libraries. Libraries such as SciPy and Pandas build directly on NumPy arrays. NumPy arrays can be made in many dimensions and data types. You can tune them to control memory consumption by controlling their data type. They are designed to be efficient with large data sets.

Questions

1. Name three differences between NumPy arrays and Python lists.

2. Given the following code, what would you expect for the final value of d2?

```
d1 = np.array([[0, 1, 3],
               [4, 2, 9]])
d2 = d1[:, 1:]
```

3. Given the following code, what would you expect for the final value of d1[0,2]?

```
d1 = np.array([[0, 1, 3],
               [4, 2, 9]])
d2 = d1[:, 1:]
d2[0,1] = 0
```

4. If you add two arrays of dimensions (1, 2, 3) and (5, 2, 1), what will be the resulting array's dimensions?

5. Use the poly1d class to model the following polynomial:

$$6x^4 + 2x^3 + 5x^2 + x - 10$$

8

SciPy

Most people use statistics like a drunk man uses a lamppost; more for support than illumination.

Andrew Lang

In This Chapter

- Math with NumPy
- Introduction to SciPy
- `scipy.misc` submodule
- `scipy.special` submodule
- `scipy.stats` submodule

Chapter 7, "NumPy," covers NumPy arrays, which are foundational building blocks for many data science–related libraries. This chapter introduces the SciPy library, which is a library for mathematics, science, and engineering.

SciPy Overview

The SciPy library is a collection of packages that build on NumPy to provide tools for scientific computing. It includes submodules that deal with optimization, Fourier transformations, signal processing, linear algebra, image processing, and statistics, among others. This chapter touches on three submodules: the `scipy.misc` submodule, the `scipy.special` submodule, and `scipy.stats`, which is the submodule most useful for data science.

This chapter also uses the library `matplotlib` for some examples. It has visualization capabilities for numerous plot types as well as images. The convention for importing its plotting library is to import it with the name `plt`:

```
import matplotlib.pyplot as plt
```

The `scipy.misc` Submodule

The `scipy.misc` submodule contains functions that don't have a home elsewhere. One fun function in this module is `scipy.misc.face()`, which can be run with this code:

```
from scipy import misc
import matplotlib.pyplot as plt
face = misc.face()
plt.imshow(face)
plt.show()
```

You can try this yourself to generate the output.

The ascent function returns a grayscale image that is available for use and demos. If you call `ascent()`, the result is a two-dimensional NumPy array:

```
a = misc.ascent()
print(a)
[[ 83  83  83 ... 117 117 117]
 [ 82  82  83 ... 117 117 117]
 [ 80  81  83 ... 117 117 117]
              ...
 [178 178 178 ...  57  59  57]
 [178 178 178 ...  56  57  57]
 [178 178 178 ...  57  57  58]]
```

If you pass this array to the `matplotlib` plot object, you see the image shown in Figure 8.1:

```
plt.imshow(a)
plt.show()
```

Figure 8.1   Demo Image from the `scipy.misc` Submodule

As you can see in this example, you use the `plt.imshow()` method to visualize images.

The `scipy.special` Submodule

The `scipy.special` submodule contains utilities for mathematical physics. It includes Airy functions, elliptical functions, Bessel functions, Struve functions, and many more. The majority of these functions support broadcasting and are compatible with NumPy arrays. To use the functions, you simply import `scipy.special` from SciPy and call the functions directly. For example, you can calculate the factorial of a number by using the `special.factorial()` function:

```
from scipy import special
special.factorial(3)
6.0
```

You can calculate the number of combinations or permutations as follows:

```
special.comb(10, 2)
45.0
```

```
special.perm(10,2)
90.0
```

This example shows 10 items and choosing 2 of them at a time.

> **Note**
>
> `scipy.special` has a `scipy.stats` submodule, but it is not meant for direct use. Rather, you use the `scipy.stats` submodule for your statistics needs. This submodule is discussed next.

The `scipy.stats` Submodule

The `scipy.stats` submodule offers probability distributions and statistical functions. The following sections take a look at just a few of the distributions offered in this submodule.

Discrete Distributions

SciPy offers some discrete distributions that share some common methods. These common methods are demonstrated in Listing 8.2 using a binomial distribution. A binomial distribution involves some number of trials, with each trial having either a success or failure outcome.

Listing 8.2   **Binomial Distribution**

```
from scipy import stats
B = stats.binom(20, 0.3) # Define a binomial distribution consisting of
                         # 20 trials and 30% chance of success

B.pmf(2) # Probability mass function (probability that a sample is equal to 2)
0.02784587252426866
```

```
B.cdf(4) # Cumulative distribution function (probability that a
         # sample is less than 4)
0.2375077788776017

B.mean # Mean of the distribution
6.0

B.var()# Variance of the distribution
4.199999999999999

B.std()# Standard deviation of the distribution
2.0493901531919194

B.rvs()# Get a random sample from the distribution
5

B.rvs(15) # Get 15 random samples
array([ 2,  8,  6,  3,  5,  5, 10,  7,  5, 10,  5,  5,  5,  2,  6])
```

If you take a large enough random sample of the distribution:

```
rvs = B.rvs(size=100000)
rvs
array([11,  4,  4, ...,  7,  6,  8])
```

You can use matplotlib to plot it and get a sense of its shape (see Figure 8.2):

```
import matplotlib.pyplot as plt
plt.hist(rvs)
plt.show()
```

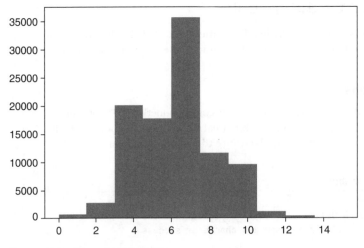

Figure 8.2   Binomial Distribution

The numbers along the bottom of the distribution in Figure 8.2 represent the number of successes in each 20-trial experiment. You can see that 6 out of 20 is the most common result, and it matches the 30% success rate.

Another distribution modeled in the `scipy.stats` submodule is the Poisson distribution. This distribution models the probability of a certain number of individual events happening across some scope of time. The shape of the distribution is controlled by its mean, which you can set by using the mu keyword. For example, a lower mean, such as 3, will skew the distribution to the left, as shown in Figure 8.3:

```
P = stats.poisson(mu=3)
rvs = P.rvs(size=10000)
rvs
array([4, 4, 2, ..., 1, 0, 2])

plt.hist(rvs)
plt.show()
```

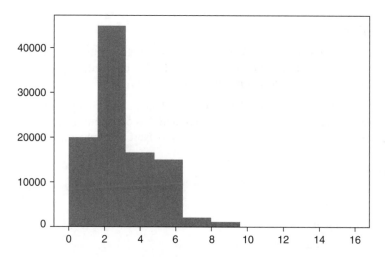

Figure 8.3   Poisson Distribution Skewed Left

A higher mean, such as 15, pushes the distribution to the right, as you can see in Figure 8.4:

```
P = stats.poisson(mu=15)
rvs = P.rvs(size=100000)
plt.hist(rvs)
plt.show()
```

Other discrete distributions modeled in the `scipy.stats` submodule include the Beta-binomial, Boltzmann (truncated Planck), Planck (discrete exponential), geometric, hypergeometric, logarithmic, and Yule–Simon, among others. At the time of this writing, there are 14 distributions modeled in the `scipy.stats` submodule.

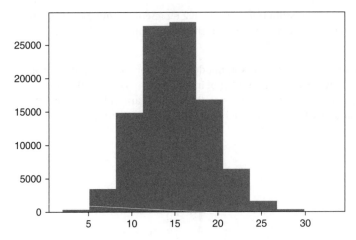

Figure 8.4   Poisson Distribution Skewed Right

Continuous Distributions

The scipy.stats submodule includes many more continuous than discrete distributions; it has 87 continuous distributions as of this writing. These distributions all take arguments for location (loc) and scale (scale). They all default to a location of 0 and scale of 1.0.

One continuous distribution modeled is the Normal distribution, which may be familiar to you as the bell curve. In this symmetric distribution, half of the data is to the left of the mean and half to the right. Here's how you can make a normal distribution using the default location and scale:

```
N = stats. norm()
rvs = N.rvs(size=100000)
plt.hist(rvs, bins=1000)
plt.show()
```

Figure 8.5 shows this distribution plotted.

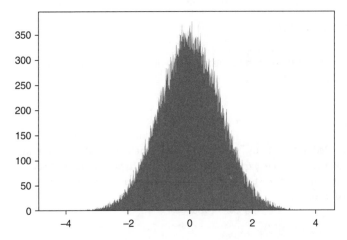

Figure 8.5   Bell Curve

You can see that the distribution is centered on 0 and is encompassed roughly between –4 and 4. Figure 8.6 shows the effects of creating a second normal distribution—this time setting the location to 30 and the scale to 50:

```
N1 = stats.norm(loc=30,scale=50)
rvs = N1.rvs(size=100000)
plt.hist(rvs, bins=1000)
plt.show()
```

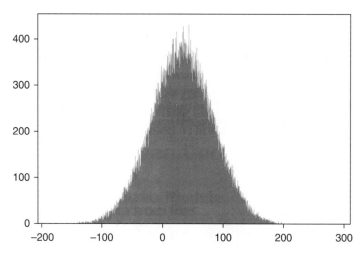

Figure 8.6   Offset Bell Curve

Notice that the distribution is now centered around 30 and encompasses a much wider range of numbers. Continuous distributions share some common functions, which are modeled in Listing 8.3. Notice that this listing uses the second Normal distribution with the offset location and greater standard deviation.

Listing 8.3   **Normal Distribution**

```
N1 = stats.norm(loc=30, scale=50)
N1.mean() # Mean of the distribution, which matches the loc value
30.0

N1.pdf(4) # Probability density function
0.006969850255179491

N1.cdf(2) # Cumulative distribution function
0.28773971884902705

N1.rvs() # A random sample
171.55168607574785
```

```
N1.var() # Variance
2500.0
```

```
N1.median()# Median
30.0
```

```
N1.std() # Standard deviation
50.0
```

> **Note**
>
> If you try the examples shown here, some of your values may differ due to random number generation.

The following continuous distribution is an exponential distribution, which is characterized by an exponentially changing curve, either up or down (see Figure 8.7):

```
E = stats.expon()
rvs = E.rvs(size=100000)
plt.hist(rvs, bins=1000)
plt.show()
```

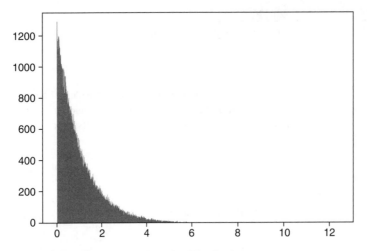

Figure 8.7   Exponentially Changing Distribution

You can see that Figure 8.7 displays a curve as you would expect from an exponential function. The following is a uniform distribution, which is has a constant probability and is also known as a rectangular distribution:

```
U = stats.uniform()
rvs = U.rvs(size=10000)
rvs
```

```
array([8.24645026e-01, 5.02358065e-01, 4.95390940e-01, ...,
       8.63031657e-01, 1.05270200e-04, 1.03627699e-01])
```

```
plt.hist(rvs, bins=1000)
plt.show()
```

This distribution gives an even probability over a set range. Its plot is shown in Figure 8.8.

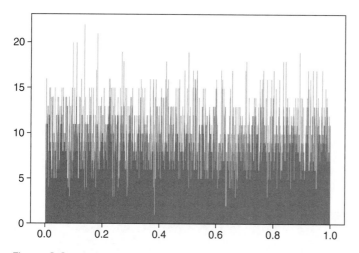

Figure 8.8   Uniform Distribution

Summary

The NumPy and SciPy libraries both offer utilities for solving complex mathematical problems. These two libraries cover a great breadth and depth of resources, and entire books have been devoted to their application. You have seen only a few of the many capabilities. These libraries are the first places you should look when you embark on solving or modeling complex mathematical problems.

Questions

1. Use the `scipy.stats` submodule to model a Normal distribution with a mean of 15.

2. Generate 25 random samples from the distribution modeled in Question 1.

3. Which scipy submodule has utilities designed for mathematical physics?

4. What method is provided with a discrete distribution to calculate its standard deviation?

9

Pandas

To clarify, *add* data.

Edward R. Tufte

In This Chapter

- Introduction to Pandas DataFrames
- Creating DataFrames
- DataFrame introspection
- Accessing data
- Manipulating DataFrames
- Manipulating DataFrame data

The Pandas DataFrame, which is built on top of the NumPy array, is probably the most commonly used data structure. DataFrames are like supercharged spreadsheets in code. They are one of the primary tools used in data science. This chapter looks at creating DataFrames, manipulating DataFrames, accessing data in DataFrames, and manipulating that data.

About DataFrames

A Pandas DataFrame, like a spreadsheet, is made up of columns and rows. Each column is a `pandas.Series` object. A DataFrame is, in some ways, similar to a two-dimensional NumPy array, with labels for the columns and index. Unlike a NumPy array, however, a DataFrame can contain different data types. You can think of a `pandas.Series` object as a one-dimensional NumPy array with labels. The `pandas.Series` object, like a NumPy array, can contain only one data type. The `pandas.Series` object can use many of the same methods you have seen with arrays, such as `min()`, `max()`, `mean()`, and `medium()`.

The usual convention is to import the Pandas package aliased as pd:

```
import pandas as pd
```

Creating DataFrames

You can create DataFrames with data from many sources, including dictionaries and lists and, more commonly, by reading files. You can create an empty DataFrame by using the `DataFrame` constructor:

```
df = pd.DataFrame()
print(df)
Empty DataFrame
Columns: []
Index: []
```

As a best practice, though, DataFrames should be initialized with data.

Creating a DataFrame from a Dictionary

You can create DataFrames from a list of dictionaries or from a dictionary, where each key is a column label with the values for that key holding the data for the column. Listing 9.1 shows how to create a DataFrame by creating a list of data for each column and then creating a dictionary with the column names as keys and these lists as the values. The listing shows how to then pass this dictionary to the DataFrame constructor to construct the DataFrame.

Listing 9.1   **Creating a DataFrame from a Dictionary**

```
first_names = ['shanda', 'rolly', 'molly', 'frank',
               'rip', 'steven', 'gwen', 'arthur']

last_names = ['smith', 'brocker', 'stein', 'bach',
              'spencer', 'de wilde', 'mason', 'davis']

ages = [43, 23, 78, 56, 26, 14, 46, 92]
data = {'first':first_names,
        'last':last_names,
        'ages':ages}

participants = pd.DataFrame(data)
```

The resulting DataFrame, `participants`, looks as follows in Colab or in a Jupyter notebook:

	first	last	ages
0	shanda	smith	43
1	rolly	brocker	23
2	molly	stein	78
3	frank	bach	56
4	rip	spencer	26
5	steven	de wilde	14
6	gwen	mason	46
7	arthur	davis	92

> **Note**
>
> In this chapter, DataFrame tables that result from a code example will be presented as a table after the code.

You can see the column labels across the top, the data in each row, and the index labels to the left.

Creating a DataFrame from a List of Lists

You can create a list of lists, with each sublist containing the data for one row, in the order of the columns:

```
data = [["shanda", "smith", 43],
        ["rolly", "brocker", 23],
        ["molly", "stein", 78],
        ["frank", "bach", 56],
        ["rip", "spencer", 26],
        ["steven", "de wilde", 14],
        ["gwen", "mason", 46],
        ["arthur", "davis", 92]]
```

Then you can use this as the data argument:

```
participants = pd.DataFrame(data)
participants
```

You get the same result as when creating a DataFrame from a dictionary:

	0	1	2
0	shanda	smith	43
1	rolly	brocker	23
2	molly	stein	78
3	frank	bach	56
4	rip	spencer	26
5	steven	de wilde	14
6	gwen	mason	46
7	arthur	davis	92

Notice that the resulting DataFrame has been created with integer column names. This is the default if no column names are supplied. You can supply column names explicitly as a list of strings:

```
column_names = ['first', 'last', 'ages']
```

Similarly, you can supply index labels as a list:

```
index_labels = ['a', 'b', 'c', 'd', 'e', 'f', 'g', 'h']
```

These labels are then used during initialization, using the parameters `columns` and `index`:

```
participants = pd.DataFrame(data,
                    columns=column_names,
                    index=index_labels)
```

	first	last	ages
a	shanda	smith	43
b	rolly	brocker	23
c	molly	stein	78
d	frank	bach	56
e	rip	spencer	26
f	steven	de wilde	14
g	gwen	mason	46
h	arthur	davis	92

Creating a DataFrame from a File

While creating DataFrames from dictionaries and lists is possible, the vast majority of the time you will create DataFrames from existing data sources. Files are the most common of these data sources. Pandas supplies functions for creating DataFrames from files for many common file types, including CSV, Excel, HTML, JSON, and SQL database connections.

Say that you want to open a CSV file from the FiveThirtyEight website, https://data.fivethirtyeight.com, under the data set `college_majors`. After you unzip and upload the CSV file to Colab, you open it by simply supplying its path to the Pandas `read_csv` function:

```
college_majors = pd.read_csv('/content/all-ages.csv')
college_majors
```

	Major	Major_category	Total	Unemployment_rate
0	GENERAL AGRICULTURE	Agriculture & Natural Resources	128148	0.026147
1	AGRICULTURE PRODUCTION AND MANAGEMENT	Agriculture & Natural Resources	95326	0.028636
2	AGRICULTURAL ECONOMICS	Agriculture & Natural Resources	33955	0.030248
...	...	...	...	...
170	MISCELLANEOUS BUSINESS & MEDICAL ADMINISTRATION	Business	102753	0.052679
171	HISTORY	Humanities & Liberal Arts	712509	0.065851
172	UNITED STATES HISTORY	Humanities & Liberal Arts	17746	0.073500

Pandas uses the data in the CSV file to determine column labels and column types.

Interacting with DataFrame Data

Once you have data loaded into a DataFrame, you should take a look at it. Pandas offers numerous ways of accessing data in a DataFrame. You can look at data by rows, columns, individual cells, or some combination of these. You can also extract data based on its value.

> **Note**
>
> When I first load data that I am unfamiliar with, I start by taking a peek at the top few rows and checking summary statistics on the data. Looking at the top rows of a DataFrame gives me a sense of what the new data looks like and allows me to confirm that the data is what I expect.

Heads and Tails

To see the top rows of a DataFrame, you can use the head method, which returns the top five rows:

```
college_majors.head()
```

	Major	Major_category	Total	Unemployment_rate
0	GENERAL AGRICULTURE	Agriculture & Natural Resources	128148	0.026147
1	AGRICULTURE PRODUCTION AND MANAGEMENT	Agriculture & Natural Resources	95326	0.028636
2	AGRICULTURAL ECONOMICS	Agriculture & Natural Resources	33955	0.030248
3	ANIMAL SCIENCES	Agriculture & Natural Resources	103549	0.042679
4	FOOD SCIENCE	Agriculture & Natural Resources	24280	0.049188

The head method takes an optional argument, which specifies the number of rows to return. You would specify the top three rows like this:

```
college_majors.head(3)
```

	Major	Major_category	Total	Unemployment_rate
0	GENERAL AGRICULTURE	Agriculture & Natural Resources	128148	0.026147
1	AGRICULTURE PRODUCTION AND MANAGEMENT	Agriculture & Natural Resources	95326	0.028636
2	AGRICULTURAL ECONOMICS	Agriculture & Natural Resources	33955	0.030248

The `tail` method works in a similar way to head but returns rows from the bottom. It also takes an optional argument that specifies the number of rows to return:

```
college_majors.tail()
```

	Major	Major_category	Total	Unemployment_rate
168	HOSPITALITY MANAGEMENT	Business	200854	0.051447
169	MANAGEMENT INFORMATION SYSTEMS AND STATISTICS	Business	156673	0.043977
170	MISCELLANEOUS BUSINESS & MEDICAL ADMINISTRATION	Business	102753	0.052679
171	HISTORY	Humanities & Liberal Arts	712509	0.065851
172	UNITED STATES HISTORY	Humanities & Liberal Arts	17746	0.073500

Descriptive Statistics

Once I've taken a look at some rows from a DataFrame, I like to get a sense of the shape of the data. One tool for doing this is the DataFrame `describe` method, which produces various descriptive statistics about the data. You can call `describe` with no arguments, as shown here:

```
college_majors.describe()
```

	Total	Unemployment_rate
count	1.730000e+02	173.000000
mean	2.302566e+05	0.057355
std	4.220685e+05	0.019177
min	2.396000e+03	0.000000
25%	2.428000e+04	0.046261
50%	7.579100e+04	0.054719
75%	2.057630e+05	0.069043
max	3.123510e+06	0.156147

This method calculates the count, mean, standard deviation, minimum, maximum, and quantiles for columns containing numeric data. It accepts optional arguments to control which data types are processed and the ranges of the quantiles returned. To change the quantiles, you use the `percentiles` argument:

```
college_majors.describe(percentiles=[0.1, 0.9])
```

	Total	Unemployment_rate
count	1.730000e+02	173.000000
mean	2.302566e+05	0.057355
std	4.220685e+05	0.019177
min	2.396000e+03	0.000000
10%	9.775600e+03	0.037053
50%	7.579100e+04	0.054719
90%	6.739758e+05	0.080062
max	3.123510e+06	0.156147

This example specifies percentiles for 10% and 90% rather than the default 25% and 75%. Note that 50% is inserted regardless of the argument.

If you want to see statistics calculated from nonnumeric columns, you can specify which data types are processed. You do this by using the `include` keyword. The value passed to this keyword should be a sequence of data types, which can be NumPy data types, such as `np.object`. In Pandas, strings are of type `object`, so the following includes columns with string data types:

```
import numpy as np
college_majors.describe(include=[np.object])
```

This would also find the string name of the data type, which, in the case of `np.object`, would be `object`. The following returns statistics appropriately for the type:

```
college_majors.describe(include=['object'])
```

So, for strings, you get the count, the number of unique values, the top value, and the frequency of this top value:

	Major	Major_category
count	173	173
unique	173	16
top	GEOSCIENCES	Engineering
freq	1	29

You can pass the string `all` instead of a list of data types to produce statistics for all the columns:

```
college_majors.describe(include='all')
```

	Major	Major_category	Total	Unemployment_rate
count	173	173	1.730000e+02	173.000000
unique	173	16	NaN	NaN
top	GEOSCIENCES	Engineering	NaN	NaN

	Major	Major_category	Total	Unemployment_rate
freq	1	29	NaN	NaN
mean	NaN	NaN	2.302566e+05	0.057355
std	NaN	NaN	4.220685e+05	0.019177
min	NaN	NaN	2.396000e+03	0.000000
25%	NaN	NaN	2.428000e+04	0.046261
50%	NaN	NaN	7.579100e+04	0.054719
75%	NaN	NaN	2.057630e+05	0.069043
max	NaN	NaN	3.123510e+06	0.156147

> **Note**
>
> Where a statistic is not appropriate for a data type, such as with the standard deviation for a string, the not-a-number value NAN is inserted.

In case you want to exclude certain data types rather than specify which ones to include, Pandas supplies the `exclude` argument, which takes the same types of arguments as `include`:

```
college_majors.describe(exclude=['int'])
```

Accessing Data

Once you have taken an initial peek at a frame using `head` or `tail` and gotten a sense of the shape of the data using `describe`, you can start looking at the data and individual columns, rows, or cells.

This is the `participants` DataFrame from earlier in the chapter:

```
participants
```

	first	last	ages
a	shanda	smith	43
b	rolly	brocker	23
c	molly	stein	78
d	frank	bach	56
e	rip	spencer	26
f	steven	de wilde	14
g	gwen	mason	46
h	arthur	davis	92

Bracket Syntax

To access columns or rows in Pandas DataFrames, you need to use bracket syntax. This syntax is great for interactive sessions where you are exploring and playing with data, and using it is a best practice.

To access a single column, you supply the column name as an argument in brackets, much as you would a dictionary key:

```
participants['first']
a    shanda
b     rolly
c     molly
d     frank
e       rip
f    steven
g      gwen
h    arthur
Name: first, dtype: object
```

You can see that this returns the data for the column along with its index, label, and data type. If a column name does not contain dashes or special characters, and if the column name is not the same as an existing attribute of the DataFrame, you can access the column as an attribute.

For example, here is how you access the ages column:

```
participants.ages
a    43
b    23
c    78
d    56
e    26
f    14
g    46
h    92
Name: ages, dtype: int64
```

This would not work with the columns first or last, as these already exist as attributes of the DataFrame.

To access multiple columns, you specify the column label as a list:

```
participants[['last', 'first']]
```

	last	first
a	smith	shanda
b	brocker	rolly
c	stein	molly
d	bach	frank
e	spencer	rip
f	de wilde	steven
g	mason	gwen

This returns a DataFrame with only the requested columns.

The bracket syntax is overloaded to allow you to grab rows as well as columns. To specify rows, you use a slice as an argument. If the slice uses integers, then those integers represent the row numbers to return. To return rows 3, 4, and 5 of the DataFrame participants, for example, you can use the slice 3:6:

`participants[3:6]`

	first	last	ages
d	frank	bach	56
e	rip	spencer	26
f	steven	de wilde	14

You can also slice using index labels. When you use labels to slice, the last value is included. So to get rows a, b, and c, you slice using a:c:

`participants['a':'c']`

	first	last	ages
a	shanda	smith	43
b	rolly	brocker	23
c	molly	stein	78

You can indicate which rows to return by using a list of Booleans. The list should have one Boolean per row: True for the desired rows, and False for the others. The following example returns the second, third, and sixth rows:

```
mask = [False, True, True, False, False, True, False, False]
participants[mask]
```

	first	last	ages
b	rolly	brocker	23
c	molly	stein	78
f	steven	de wilde	14

The bracket syntax provides a very convenient and easy-to-read way to access data. It is often used in interactive sessions when experimenting with and exploring DataFrames, but it is not optimized for performance with large data sets. The recommended way to index into DataFrames in production code or for large data sets is to use the DataFrame loc and iloc indexers. These indexers use a bracket syntax very similar to what you have seen here. The loc indexer indexes using labels, and iloc uses index positions.

Optimized Access by Label

With the loc indexer, you can supply a single label, and the values for that row will be returned. To get the values from the row labeled c, for example, you simply supply c as an argument:

```
participants.loc['c']
first    molly
last     stein
ages        78
Name: c, dtype: object
```

You can provide a slice of labels, and once again, the last label is included:

```
participants.loc['c':'f']
```

	first	last	ages
c	molly	stein	78
d	frank	bach	56
e	rip	spencer	26
f	steven	de wilde	14

Or you can provide a sequence of Booleans:

```
mask = [False, True, True, False, False, True, False, False]
participants.loc[mask]
```

	first	last	ages
b	rolly	brocker	23
c	molly	stein	78
f	steven	de wilde	14

An optional second argument can indicate which columns to return. If you want to return all the rows for the column first, for example, you specify all rows with a slice, a comma, and the column label:

```
participants.loc[:, 'first']
a    shanda
b     rolly
c     molly
d     frank
e       rip
f    steven
g      gwen
h    arthur
Name: first, dtype: object
```

You could provide a list of column labels:

```
participants.loc[:'c', ['ages', 'last']]
```

	ages	last
a	43	smith
b	23	brocker
c	78	stein

Or you could provide a list of Booleans:

```
participants.loc[:'c', [False, True, True]]
```

	last	ages
a	smith	43
b	brocker	23
c	stein	78

Optimized Access by Index

The iloc indexer enables you to use index positions to select rows and columns. Much as you've seen before with brackets, you can use a single value to specify a single row:

```
participants.iloc[3]
first     frank
last      bach
ages        56
Name: d, dtype: object
```

Or you can specify multiple rows by using a slice:

```
participants.iloc[1:4]
```

	first	last	ages
b	rolly	brocker	23
c	molly	stein	78
d	frank	bach	56

You can, optionally, indicate which column to return by using a second slice:

```
participants.iloc[1:4, :2]
```

	first	last
b	rolly	brocker
c	molly	stein
d	frank	bach

Masking and Filtering

A powerful feature of DataFrames is the ability to select data based on values. You can use comparison operators with columns to see which values meet some condition. For example, if you want to see which rows of the college_majors DataFrame have the value Humanities & Liberal Arts as a major category, you can use the equality operator (==):

```
college_majors.Major_category == 'Humanities & Liberal Arts'
0       False
1       False
2       False
3       False
        ...
169     False
170     False
171      True
172      True
Name: Major_category, Length: 173, dtype: bool
```

This produces a pandas.Series object that contains True for every row that matches the condition. A series of Booleans is mildly interesting, but the real power comes when you combine it with an indexer to filter the results. Remember that loc returns rows for every True value of an input sequence. You can make a condition based on a comparison operator and a row, for example, as shown here for the greater-than operator and the row Total:

```
total_mask = college_majors.loc[:, 'Total'] > 1200000
```

You can use the result as a mask to select only the rows that meet this condition:

```
top_majors = college_majors.loc[total_mask]
top_majors
```

	Major	Major_category	Total	Unemployment_rate
25	GENERAL EDUCATION	Education	1438867	0.043904
28	ELEMENTARY EDUCATION	Education	1446701	0.038359
114	PSYCHOLOGY	Psychology & Social Work	1484075	0.069667
153	NURSING	Health	1769892	0.026797
158	GENERAL BUSINESS	Business	2148712	0.051378
159	ACCOUNTING	Business	1779219	0.053415
161	BUSINESS MANAGEMENT AND ADMINISTRATION	Business	3123510	0.058865

You can use the min() method to check whether the resulting DataFrame meets the condition:

```
top_majors.Total.min()
1438867
```

Now say that you want to see which major categories have the lowest unemployment rates. You can use `describe` on a single column as well as with a full DataFrame. If you use `describe` on the column `Unemployment_rate`, for example, you can see that the top rate for the bottom percentile is 0.046261:

```
college_majors.Unemployment_rate.describe()
count    173.000000
mean       0.057355
std        0.019177
min        0.000000
25%        0.046261
50%        0.054719
75%        0.069043
max        0.156147
Name: Unemployment_rate, dtype: float64
```

You can create a mask for all rows with an unemployment rate less than or equal to this:

```
employ_rate_mask = college_majors.loc[:, 'Unemployment_rate'] <= 0.046261
```

And you can use this mask to produce a DataFrame with only these rows:

```
employ_rate_majors = college_majors.loc[employ_rate_mask]
```

Then you can use the `pandas.Series` object's `unique` method to see which major categories are in the resulting DataFrame:

```
employ_rate_majors.Major_category.unique()
array(['Agriculture & Natural Resources', 'Education', 'Engineering',
       'Biology & Life Science', 'Computers & Mathematics',
       'Humanities & Liberal Arts', 'Physical Sciences', 'Health',
       'Business'], dtype=object)
```

All these categories have at least one row with an employment rate that meets the condition.

Pandas Boolean Operators

You can use the three Boolean operators AND (&), OR (|), and NOT (~) with the results of your conditions. You can use & or | to combine conditions and create more complex ones. You can use ~ to create a mask that is the opposite of your condition.

For example, you can use AND to create a new mask based on the previous ones to see which major categories of the most popular majors have a low unemployment rate. To do this, you use the & operator between your existing masks to produce a new one:

```
total_rate_mask = employ_rate_mask & total_mask
total_rate_mask
0    False
1    False
2    False
3    False
4    False
    ...
```

```
168     False
169     False
170     False
171     False
172     False
Length: 173, dtype: bool
```

By looking at the resulting DataFrame, you can see which of the most popular majors have the lowest unemployment rates:

```
college_majors.loc[total_rate_mask]
```

	Major	Major_category	Total	Unemployment_rate
25	GENERAL EDUCATION	Education	1438867	0.043904
28	ELEMENTARY EDUCATION	Education	1446701	0.038359
153	NURSING	Health	1769892	0.026797

You can use the ~ operator with your employment rate mask to create a DataFrame whose rows all have an employment rate higher than the bottom percentile:

```
lower_rate_mask = ~employ_rate_mask
lower_rate_majors = college_majors.loc[lower_rate_mask]
```

You can check this work by using the min method on the Unemployment_rate column to see that it is above the top rate for the bottom percentile:

```
lower_rate_majors.Unemployment_rate.min()
0.046261360999999994
```

To select all the rows that either fit the top majors condition or the employment rate condition, you can use the | operator:

```
college_majors.loc[total_mask | employ_rate_mask]
```

The resulting DataFrame contains all the rows that fit either condition.

Manipulating DataFrames

Once you have the data you need in a DataFrame, you might want to change the DataFrame. You can rename columns or indexes, you can add new columns and rows, and you can delete columns and rows.

Changing the label of a column is simple using the DataFrame rename method. This is how you can use the DataFrame columns attribute to look at the current column names:

```
participants.columns
Index(['first', 'last', 'ages'], dtype='object')
```

You can then rename the columns of your choice by providing a dictionary mapping each old column name to the new one. For example, here is how you change the label of the column ages to Age:

```
participants.rename(columns={'ages': 'Age'})
```

	first	last	Age
a	shanda	smith	43
b	rolly	brocker	23
c	molly	stein	78
d	frank	bach	56
e	rip	spencer	26
f	steven	de wilde	14
g	gwen	mason	46
h	arthur	davis	92

By default, the rename method returns a new DataFrame using the new column labels. So, if you check your original DataFrame's column names again, you see the old column name:

```
participants.columns
Index(['first', 'last', 'ages'], dtype='object')
```

This is how many DataFrame methods work (preserving the original state). Many of these methods offer an optional inplace argument, which, if set to True, changes the original DataFrame:

```
participants.rename(columns={'ages':'Age'}, inplace=True)
participants.columns

Index(['first', 'last', 'Age'], dtype='object')
```

You can use the indexer syntax to create new columns. To do so, you simply access the column as if it already exists by using an indexer and the cited values:

```
participants['Zip Code'] = [94702, 97402, 94223, 94705,
                            97503, 94705, 94111, 95333]

participants
```

	first	last	Age	Zip Code
a	shanda	smith	43	94702
b	rolly	brocker	23	97402
c	molly	stein	78	94223
d	frank	bach	99	94705
e	rip	spencer	26	97503
f	steven	de wilde	14	94705
g	gwen	mason	46	94111
h	arthur	davis	92	95333

You can use operations between columns such as string addition to create values for a new column. If you decide you want to add a column with participants' full names, you can construct the values from the existing columns for their first and last names:

```
participants['Full Name'] = ( participants.loc[:, 'first'] +
                              participants.loc[:, 'last'] )
```

participants

	first	last	Age	Zip Code	Full Name
a	shanda	smith	43	94702	shandasmith
b	rolly	brocker	23	97402	rollybrocker
c	molly	stein	78	94223	mollystein
d	frank	bach	99	94705	frankbach
e	rip	spencer	26	97503	ripspencer
f	steven	de wilde	14	94705	stevende wilde
g	gwen	mason	46	94111	gwenmason
h	arthur	davis	92	95333	arthurdavis

You can update a column by using the same syntax. For example, if you decide that the values in the full name column should have a white space between the names, you can just assign new values by using the same column name:

```
participants['Full Name'] = ( participants.loc[:, 'first'] +
                              ' ' +
                              participants.loc[:, 'last'] )
```
participants

	first	last	Age	Zip Code	Full Name
a	shanda	smith	43	94702	shanda smith
b	rolly	brocker	23	97402	rolly brocker
c	molly	stein	78	94223	molly stein
d	frank	bach	99	94705	frank bach
e	rip	spencer	26	97503	rip spencer
f	steven	de wilde	14	94705	steven de wilde
g	gwen	mason	46	94111	gwen mason
h	arthur	davis	92	95333	arthur davis

Manipulating Data

Pandas gives you many ways to change data in a DataFrame. You can set values by using the same indexers you used before. You can do operations on whole DataFrames or on individual columns.

And you can apply functions to change elements in a column or create new values from multiple rows or columns.

To change data using an indexer, you select the location where you want the new data to reside in the same way you select to view data, and then you assign a new value. To change `arthur` in column h to `Paul`, for example, you can use `loc`:

```
participants.loc['h', 'first'] = 'Paul'
participants
```

	first	last	Age	Zip Code	Full Name
a	shanda	smith	43	94702	shanda smith
b	rolly	brocker	23	97402	rolly brocker
c	molly	stein	78	94223	molly stein
d	frank	bach	99	94705	frank bach
e	rip	spencer	26	97503	rip spencer
f	steven	de wilde	14	94705	steven de wilde
g	gwen	mason	46	94111	gwen mason
h	paul	davis	92	95333	arthur davis

Alternatively, you can use `iloc` to set the age of Molly in row c to 99:

```
participants.iloc[3, 2] = 99
participants
```

	first	last	Age	Zip Code	Full Name
a	shanda	smith	43	94702	shanda smith
b	rolly	brocker	23	97402	rolly brocker
c	molly	stein	78	94223	molly stein
d	frank	bach	99	94705	frank bach
e	rip	spencer	26	97503	rip spencer
f	steven	de wilde	14	94705	steven de wilde
g	gwen	mason	46	94111	gwen mason
h	paul	davis	92	95333	arthur davis

This should seem fairly intuitive if you think of it as a variation on the indexed assignment you have used with lists and dictionaries.

Earlier in this chapter, you used operations between columns to construct values for a new column. You can also use in-place operators such as +=, -=, and /= , to change values in a column. To subtract 1 from the age of each participant, for example, you can use the -= operator:

```
participants.Age -= 1
participants
```

	first	last	Age	Zip Code	Full Name
a	shanda	smith	42	94702	shanda smith
b	rolly	brocker	22	97402	rolly brocker
c	molly	stein	77	94223	molly stein
d	frank	bach	98	94705	frank bach
e	rip	spencer	25	97503	rip spencer
f	steven	de wilde	13	94705	steven de wilde
g	gwen	mason	45	94111	gwen mason
h	paul	davis	91	95333	arthur davis

The `replace` Method

The `replace` method finds and replaces values across a DataFrame. For example, you can use it to replace the name `rolly` with `Smiley`:

```
participants.replace('rolly', 'Smiley')
```

	first	last	Age	Zip Code	Full Name
a	shanda	smith	42	94702	shanda smith
b	smiley	brocker	22	97402	rolly brocker
c	molly	stein	77	94223	molly stein
d	frank	bach	98	94705	frank bach
e	rip	spencer	25	97503	rip spencer
f	steven	de wilde	13	94705	steven de wilde

. . .

This method also works with regular expressions. Here is how you construct a regular expression that matches words starting with s and replaces the s with S:

```
participants.replace(r'(s)([a-z]+)', r'S\2', regex=True)
```

	first	last	Age	Zip Code	Full Name
a	shanda	smith	42	94702	Shanda Smith
b	rolly	brocker	22	97402	rolly brocker
c	molly	stein	77	94223	molly Stein
d	frank	bach	98	94705	frank bach
e	rip	spencer	25	97503	rip Spencer

	first	last	Age	Zip Code	Full Name
f	steven	de wilde	13	94705	Steven de wilde
g	gwen	mason	45	94111	gwen mason
h	paul	davis	91	95333	arthur davis

Both DataFrames and the pandas.Series object have an apply() method that can call a function on values. In the case of a pandas.Series object, the apply() method calls a function of your choosing on every value in the pandas.Series object individually.

Say that you define a function that capitalizes any string passed to it:

```
def cap_word(w):
    return w.capitalize()
```

Then, if you pass it as an argument to apply() on the column first, it capitalizes each first name:

```
participants.loc[:, 'first'].apply(cap_word)
a     Shanda
b      Rolly
c      Molly
d      Frank
e        Rip
f     Steven
g       Gwen
h       Paul
Name: first, dtype: object
```

In the case of a DataFrame, apply takes a row as an argument, enabling you to produce new values from the columns of that row. Say that you define a function that uses values from the columns first and Age:

```
def say_hello(row):
    return f'{row["first"]} is {row["Age"]} years old.'
```

You can then apply the function to the whole DataFrame:

```
participants.apply(say_hello, axis=1)
a     shanda is 42 years old.
b      rolly is 22 years old.
c      molly is 77 years old.
d      frank is 98 years old.
e        rip is 25 years old.
f     steven is 13 years old.
g       gwen is 45 years old.
h       paul is 91 years old.
dtype: object
```

You can use this method to call a function across rows or across columns. You use the axis argument to indicate whether your function should expect a row or a column.

Interactive Display

If you are working with DataFrames in Colab, you should try running this snippet:

```
%load_ext google.colab.data_table
```

This makes the output of your DataFrames interactive and enables you to filter and select interactively.

Summary

A Pandas DataFrame is a powerful tool for working with data in a spreadsheet-like environment. You can create DataFrames from many sources, but creating a DataFrame from a file is the most common. You can extend DataFrames with new columns and rows. You can access the data itself by using powerful indexers, which you can also use to set data. DataFrames provide a great way to explore and manipulate data.

Questions

Use this table to answer the following questions:

Sample Size (mg)	%P	%Q
0.24	40	60
2.34	34	66
0.0234	12	88

1. Create a DataFrame representing this table.

2. Add a new column labeled Total Q that contains the amount of Q (in mg) for each sample.

3. Divide the columns %P and %Q by 100.

Visualization Libraries

The greatest value of a picture is when it forces us to notice what we never expected to see.

John Tukey

In This Chapter

- Creating and styling plots with `matplotlib`
- Plotting with Seaborn and Seaborn themes
- Plots with Plotly and Bokeh

Visualizing data is essential to exploring and presenting data. The saying "a picture is worth a thousand words" certainly applies to understanding data. You can often gain insights from visualizations that are not obvious from summary statistics. The statistician Francis Anscombe famously created four data sets whose summary statistics were nearly identical but that varied greatly when plotted.

Explaining your data is also often easier when you have visuals. Think about how effective charts and plots are in presentations. Luckily, there are quite a few libraries in Python designed for visualization.

`matplotlib`

`matplotlib` is a bedrock tool for creating publication-ready charts. It is used extensively on its own and also as the basis of other plotting libraries. It is part of the SciPy ecosystem, along with NumPy and Pandas. It is a very large project with wide-ranging capabilities, but because of this size, it can be complicated to use.

There are multiple interfaces for using `matplotlib`. One interface you may see if you search online, especially in older examples, is `pylab`, which is generally imported like this:

```
from matplotlib.pylab import *
```

While those older examples may have some use, the use of `pylab` is now discouraged. It was originally intended to simulate an environment similar to that of MATPLOT, which is a non-Python mathematical plotting tool. But importing all of the contents of a module—which is what happens with `import *`—is generally seen as a bad practice in Python. The recommended practice is to explicitly import only what you will use.

The recommended interface for `matplotlib` is pyplot, which is by convention aliased as `plt`:

```
import matplotlib.pyplot as plt
```

Two main concepts in `matplotlib` are figures and axes. *Figures* are used to graph data. *Axes* are areas where points can be specified using coordinates. Axes are visualized using figures. A single figure may have multiple axes, but an axis can be attached to only a single figure.

`matplotlib` offers two approaches to creating figures and axes: Create them explicitly or implicitly. The following examples show the implicit approach.

There are some plotting methods, such as `plt.plot` and `plt.hist`, that plot to the current axis and figure. These methods create an axis and a parent figure if it doesn't already exist.

The method `plt.plot` creates a line plot based on x and y values, as shown in Figure 10.1:

```
[X = [0, 1, 2, 3, 4, 5, 7, 8, 9, 10]
Y = [20, 25, 35, 50, 10, 12, 20, 40, 70, 110]
plt.plot(X, Y)
```

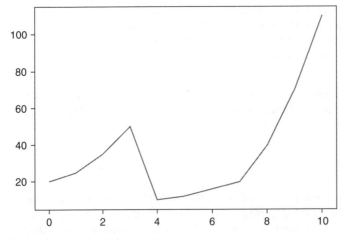

Figure 10.1   Line Plot Based on x and y Values

Styling Plots

You can control the style of a plot by using two different mechanisms. One is to use any of the properties of the `matplotlib.Line2D` class. These properties control the markers used in the plot, the style of the line, and the color. You can find a full list of `matplotlib.Line2D` properties in the `matplotlib` documentation (see https://matplotlib.org/3.3.3/api/_as_gen/matplotlib.lines.Line2D.html).

You can use these properties as keyword arguments to `plt.plot`. This section demonstrates the use of the `marker`, `linestyle`, and `color` properties.

The available marker types are as follows:

.	point marker
,	pixel marker
o	circle marker
v	triangle_down marker
^	triangle_up marker
<	triangle_left marker
>	triangle_right marker
1	tri_down marker
2	tri_up marker
3	tri_left marker
4	tri_right marker
s	square marker
p	pentagon marker
*	star marker
h	hexagon1 marker
H	hexagon2 marker
+	plus marker
x	x marker
D	diamond marker
d	thin_diamond marker
		vline marker
_	hline marker

You can specify a marker type by using the keyword `marker`. This example sets the markers as squares (see Figure 10.2):

```
X = [0, 1, 2, 3, 4, 5, 7, 8, 9, 10]
Y = [20, 25, 35, 50, 10, 12, 20, 40, 70, 110]
plt.plot(X, Y, marker='s')
```

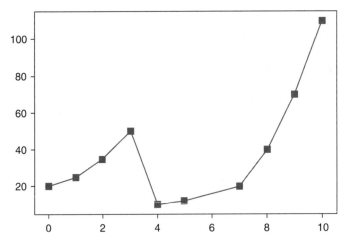

Figure 10.2   Markers as Squares Plot

These are the available line styles:

-        solid line style
- -   dashed line style
- .   dash-dot line style
:   dotted line style

You can use the keyword linestyle to set the line style (see Figure 10.3):

```
X = [0, 1, 2, 3, 4, 5, 7, 8, 9, 10]
Y = [20, 25, 35, 50, 10, 12, 20, 40, 70, 110]
plt.plot(X, Y, marker='s', linestyle=':')
```

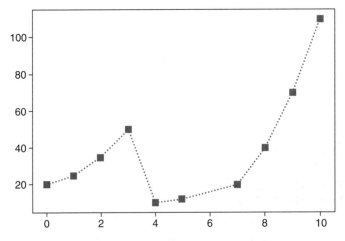

Figure 10.3   Parameter Set with the Keyword linestyle

These are the available colors:

b	blue
g	green
r	red
c	cyan
m	magenta
y	yellow
k	black
w	white

You can set the color by using the `color` keyword. If you try this example, you will see the same plot as Figure 10.3, but with color:

```
X = [0, 1, 2, 3, 4, 5, 7, 8, 9, 10]
Y = [20, 25, 35, 50, 10, 12, 20, 40, 70, 110]
plt.plot(X, Y, marker='s', linestyle=':', color='m')
```

An alternative way to set style properties is to use the `fmt` argument. This is a position parameter that appears to the right of the Y parameter. It consists of a format string that uses a shorthand for marker, line style, and color settings. The format string is of the form `[marker][line][color]`, with all the sections being optional. For example, for the plot in Figure 10.4, you can set the markers to squares, the line style to dashed, and the color to red by using the format string `s-.r`:

```
X = [0, 1, 2, 3, 4, 5, 7, 8, 9, 10]
Y = [20, 25, 35, 50, 10, 12, 20, 40, 70, 110]
fmt = 's-.r'
plt.plot(X, Y, fmt)
```

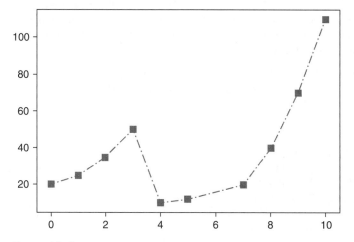

Figure 10.4   Line Plot Using the Format String `s-.r`

You can use a format string and a keyword argument together. For example, the plot in Figure 10.5 combines the format string 's-.r' with the keyword linewidth:

```
X = [0, 1, 2, 3, 4, 5, 7, 8, 9, 10]
Y = [20, 25, 35, 50, 10, 12, 20, 40, 70, 110]
fmt = 's-.r'
plt.plot(X, Y, fmt, linewidth=4.3)
```

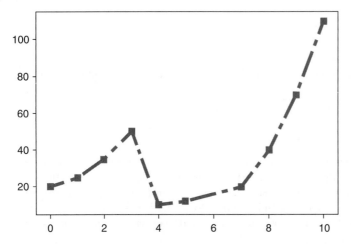

Figure 10.5   Line Plot Formatted with the Keyword linewidth

Labeled Data

matplotlib's plotting functions can use labeled data, including Pandas DataFrames, dictionaries, and pretty much any data structure for which data is accessed using bracket syntax. Instead of supplying a sequence of values for x and y, you supply the appropriate labels.

Here is how you could create a DataFrame of U.S. men's and women's average heights over a 16-year period, based on Centers for Disease Control and Prevention data (see https:// www.cdc.gov/nchs/data/nhsr/nhsr122-508.pdf):

```
import pandas as pd

data = {"Years": ["2000", "2002", "2004", "2006", "2008",
                  "2010", "2012", "2014", "2016"],
        "Men": [189.1, 191.8, 193.5, 196.0, 194.7,
                196.3, 194.4, 197.0, 197.8],
        "Women": [175.7, 176.4, 176.5, 176.2, 175.9,
                  175.9, 175.7, 175.8, 175.3]}
heights_df = pd.DataFrame(data)
```

You can create a line plot of women's heights by specifying the labels of the columns to use for x and y, as well as the DataFrame from which to pull the data (see Figure 10.6):

```
plt.plot('Years', 'Women', data=heights_df)
```

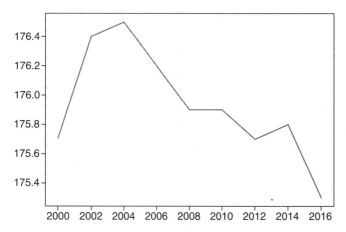

Figure 10.6   Line Plot with x and y Labels Specified

Plotting Multiple Sets of Data

There are three approaches to plotting multiple sets of data on the same chart. The first is to just call the plotting function multiple times:

```
X = [0, 1, 2, 3, 4, 5, 7, 8, 9, 10]
Y = [20, 25, 35, 50, 10, 12, 20, 40, 70, 110]
fmt = 's-.r'

X1 = [0, 1, 2, 3, 4, 5, 7, 8, 9, 10]
Y2 = [90, 89, 87, 82, 72, 60, 45, 28, 10, 0]
fmt2 = '^k:'
plt.plot(X, Y, fmt)
plt.plot(X1, Y2, fmt2)
```

Remember that plt.plot uses the current axis and figure. This means that multiple calls will continue sharing the same figure and plot. You can see multiple plots on the same figure in Figure 10.7.

The second way to plot multiple sets of data on the same chart is to pass multiple data sets to the plotting function directly:

```
plt.plot(X, Y, fmt, X1, Y2, fmt2)
```

For labeled data, you can pass multiple labels, and each column will be added to the chart (see Figure 10.8):

```
plt.plot('Years', 'Women', 'Men', data=heights_df)
```

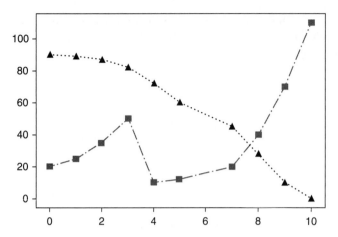

Figure 10.7   Multiple Plots on the Same Figure

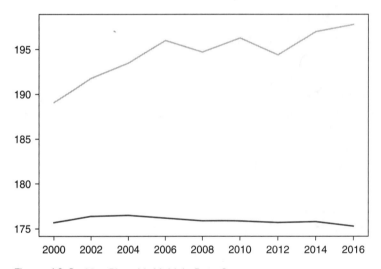

Figure 10.8   Line Plot with Multiple Data Sets

matplotlib offers convenience functions to add labels, a title, and a chart legend. You can create a labeled version of the plot from Figure 10.8 as follows (see Figure 10.9):

```
plt.plot('Years', 'Women', 'Men', data=heights_df)
plt.xlabel('Year')
plt.ylabel('Height (Inches)')
plt.title("Heights over time")
plt.legend(['Women', 'Men'])
```

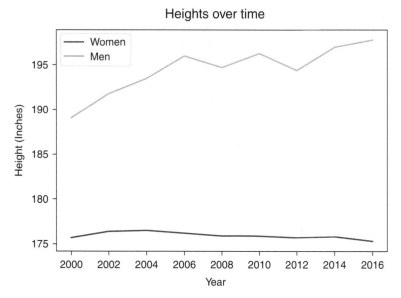

Figure 10.9   Adding Multiple Labels to a Plot

Object-Oriented Style

The implicit way of dealing with figures and axes that you have seen up to this point in the chapter is a handy way to explore data, especially in an interactive environment. matplotlib also enables you to deal with figures and axes directly, which gives you more control. The plt.subplots() function returns a figure and as many axes as you specify. You can then plot on the axes in much the same way as when using implicit plotting:

```
fig, ax = plt.subplots()
ax.plot('Years', 'Women', 'Men', data=heights_df)
ax.set_xlabel('Year')
ax.set_ylabel('Height (Inches)')
ax.set_title("Heights over time")
ax.legend(['Women', 'Men'])
```

The results will match those plotted using the same data in Figure 10.9.

If you want to make multiple charts on the same figure, you can specify multiple axes, as shown in Listing 10.1. The first argument specifies the number of rows, and the second argument speci-fies the number of columns. Figure 10.10 shows an example of creating two axes on a figure.

Listing 10.1   **Creating Multiple Axes**

```
fig, (ax1, ax2) = plt.subplots(1, 2).        # Create one figure and two axes

ax1.plot('Years', 'Women', data=heights_df)  # Plot women by years on axis one
ax1.set_xlabel('Year')                       # Label the x axis of the first axis
```

```
ax1.set_ylabel('Height (Inches)')        # Label the y axis of the first axis
ax1.set_title("Women")                    # Set the title of the first axis
ax1.legend(['Women'])                     # Set the legend of the first axis

ax2.plot('Years', 'Men', data=heights_df ) # Plot the second axis
ax2.set_xlabel('Year')                    # Set the x label for the second axis
ax2.set_title("Men")                      # Set the title for the second axis
ax2.legend(['Men'])                       # Set the legend for the second axis

fig.autofmt_xdate(rotation=65)            # Rotate the date labels
```

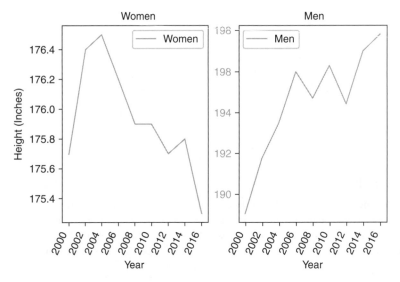

Figure 10.10   Plotting Two Axes on a Figure

The implicit style of plotting is great for exploring data in an interactive mode. The explicit style gives you much more control and is generally recommended for plotting in production code.

Seaborn

Seaborn is a statistical plotting library that is built on top of matplotlib. It is designed to make creating good-looking statistics graphics easily, and is known, among other things, for having a default style that is generally better looking than other libraries offer.

By convention, Seaborn is imported as sns:

```
import seaborn as sns
```

Seaborn includes a series of sample data sets that are used in the provided documentation and tutorials. These data sets also provide a convenient source of data when exploring Seaborn's features. You load the data sets as Pandas DataFrames, using the function `sns.load_dataset()`, with the name of the data set as an argument. The available data sets are listed at https://github.com/mwaskom/seaborn-data.

This example shows how to load up a data set of car crashes and then select the columns to work with:

```
car_crashes = sns.load_dataset('car_crashes')
car_crashes = car_crashes[['total', 'not_distracted', 'alcohol']]
```

This example uses Seaborn's `sns.relplot()` function to plot the relationship between two columns (see Figure 10.11):

```
sns.relplot(data=car_crashes,
            x='total',
            y='not_distracted')
```

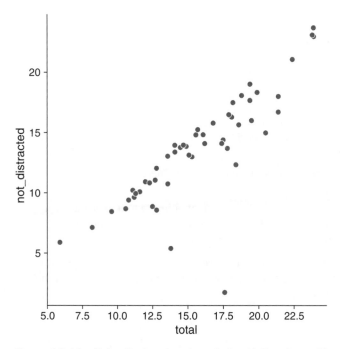

Figure 10.11   Using Seaborn's `sns.relplot()` Function to Plot the Relationship Between Two Columns

Seaborn Themes

Using Seaborn themes is an easy way to control the look of charts. To use Seaborn's default theme, you can use the following function:

```
sns.set_theme()
```

You can replot the data to see the new look shown in Figure 10.12:

```
sns.relplot(data=car_crashes,
            x='total',
            y='not_distracted')
```

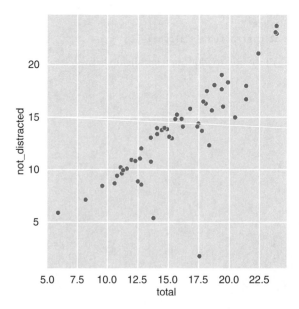

Figure 10.12   Using Seaborn Themes to Control the Look of the Chart

When you set a Seaborn theme, it is applied to any subsequent plots, even those made using matplotlib directly. Seaborn groups matplotlib parameters into two groups: one dealing with the aesthetic style of a plot and the other with scale elements.

Five preset Seaborn style themes are available: darkgrid, whitegrid, dark, white, and ticks. You can set the style by using the sns.set_style() function. For example, you could set the dark style as follows (see Figure 10.13):

```
sns.set_style('dark')
sns.relplot(data=car_crashes,
            x='total',
            y='not_distracted')
```

The themes available for setting the scale of figure elements are based on the target presentation. They are paper, notebook, talk, and poster.

You set a theme by using the sns.set_context function:

```
sns.set_context('talk')
```

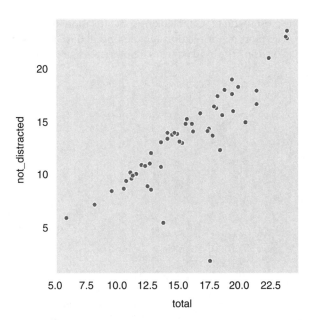

Figure 10.13   Using the Dark Style Theme

If you replot the data, the scale is adjusted, as shown in Figure 10.14:

```
sns.relplot(data=car_crashes,
            x='total',
            y='not_distracted')
```

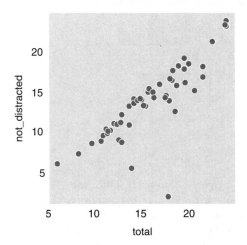

Figure 10.14   Data Replotted Using the `sns.set_context` Function

Seaborn offers many plot types. One of the most useful types for looking for correlation in data is `sns.pairplot()`, which creates a grid of axes plotting the relationships among all the columns of the DataFrame. You can create a pairplot by using the iris data set as follows (see Figure 10.15):

```
df = sns.load_dataset('iris')
sns.pairplot(df, hue='species')
```

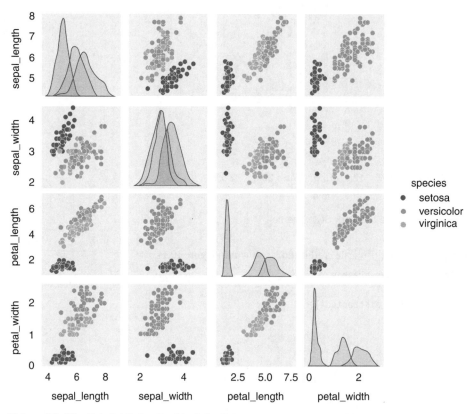

Figure 10.15   Pairplot Using the Iris Data Set

Plotly

`matplotlib` and Seaborn are excellent tools for creating publication-ready static charts. Both of them can be extended to create interactive data presentations. However, the libraries Plotly and Bokeh are specifically designed for the creation of high-quality interactive charts. Plotly offers many chart types, but one way it stands out is that it makes it easy to build 3D charts. Figure 10.16 shows a static version of a dynamic plot. If you run this code in a notebook, you will be able to rotate and zoom with that plot:

```
import plotly.express as px
iris = px.data.iris()
```

```
fig = px.scatter_3d(iris,
                    x='sepal_length',
                    y='petal_width',
                    z='petal_length',
                    color='species')
fig.show()
```

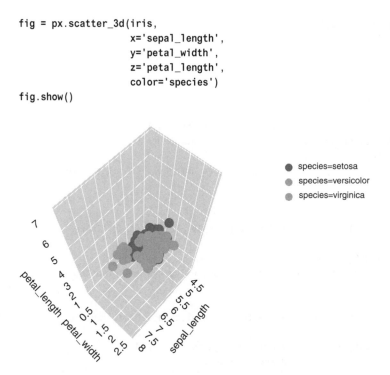

Figure 10.16   Static Version of a Dynamic Plot

Bokeh

Bokeh is an alternative to Plotly for easily creating interactive graphics. One way that Bokeh stands out is in its use of the special data object `ColumnDataSource`. This object offers improved performance and allows, among other things, the data to be updated or appended without requiring a reload of the state. The data source can also be shared across figures so that interaction with the data in one figure modifies the data in another figure. Listing 10.2 sets up multiple figures sharing a data object, and Figure 10.17 shows the result.

> **Note**
>
> Be forewarned that Bokeh requires extra setup in Colab. This example gives you an idea of Bokeh's capabilities but does not show you how to get it to plot in Colab.

Listing 10.2   **Bokeh Shared Data**

```
from bokeh.io import output_notebook
from bokeh.plotting import figure, show
from bokeh.models import ColumnDataSource
from bokeh.layouts import gridplot
```

```
Y = [x for x in range(0,200, 2)]
Y1 = [x**2 for x in Y]
X = [x for x in range(100)]
data={'x':X,
      'y':Y,
      'y1':Y1}

TOOLS = "box_select"                  # Select interactive tools
source = ColumnDataSource(data=data)  # Create ColumnDataSource
left = figure(tools=TOOLS,
              title='Brushing')       # Create figure using the selected tools

left.circle('x',
            'y',
            source=source)           # Create a circle plot on first figure

right = figure(tools=TOOLS,
               title='Brushing')     # Create figure using the selected tools
right.circle('x',
             'y1',
             source=source)          # Create circle plot on second figure

p = gridplot([[left, right]])        # Put the figures on a grid
show(p)                              # Show the grid
```

The figures that are output allow for cross-axes selection, as defined by the chosen tool. This means that if you select a section of one plot, the corresponding points of the second plot are also selected.

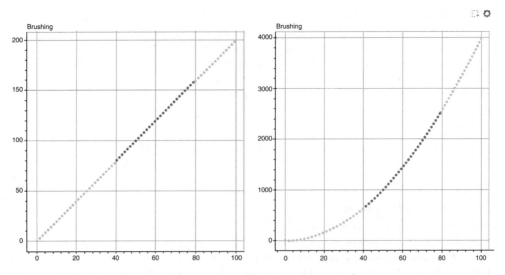

Figure 10.17   Multiple Figures Sharing a Data Object

Other Visualization Libraries

There are many other great visualization libraries in addition to the ones described so far in this chapter. Here are some others you may want to explore:

- `geoplotlib`: Enables visualization of maps and geographic data

- `ggplot`: Based on the R language package ggplot2

- `pygal`: Allows you to easily create simple plots

- `folium`: Enables you to create interactive maps

- `missingno`: Enables visualization of missing data

Summary

Visualization is an extremely useful part of data exploration and an important part of data presentation. There are many libraries available for visualizing data, all with different specialties and focuses. `matplotlib` is the base for many other libraries. It offers wide capabilities but a steep learning curve. Seaborn is a statistics visualization library built on `matplotlib` that makes it easy to improve the look of plots and to create plots for different target media. Plotly and Bokeh are both designed for the creation of interactive charts and dashboards.

Questions

Use this example to answer the following questions:

```
import matplotlib.pyplot as plt
import seaborn as sns
import pandas as pd

data = {'X'  : [x for x in range(50)],
        'Y'  : [y for y in range(50, 0, -1)],
        'Y1' : [y**2 for y in range(25, 75)]}
```

df = pd.DataFrame(data)

1. Use `matplotlib` to plot the relationship between columns X and Y.

2. Use `matplotlib` to add the relationship between columns X and Y1 to the same plot.

3. Use `matplotlib` to plot the relationships from Questions 1 and 2 on separate axes of the same figure.

4. Use Seaborn to change the theme to `darkgrid` and then repeat the plots from Question 3.

11

Machine Learning Libraries

To call in the statistician after the experiment is done may be no more than asking him to perform a post-mortem examination: he may be able to say what the experiment died of.

Ronald Fisher

In This Chapter

- Overview of popular machine learning libraries
- Introduction to Scikit-learn
- Overview of the machine learning process

Machine learning consists of letting a computer find a way to solve a problem using data. In contrast, with traditional programming, the programmer defines, in code, the way to find a solution, rather than the solution itself. This chapter provides a brief overview of some of the popular libraries used for machine learning. These libraries implement the algorithms used to create and train machine learning models. These models have various uses, depending on the type of problem. For example, some models are useful for predicting future values, and others are useful for classifying data into groups or categories.

Popular Machine Learning Libraries

Four of the most popular machine learning libraries are TensorFlow, Keras, PyTorch, and Scikit-learn:

- **TensorFlow:** Google developed this powerful library for internal use. It is used to solve problems using deep learning. This involves defining layers that transform the data and that are tuned as the solution is fit to data.

- **Keras:** This open-source library was designed to work with TensorFlow, and it is now included in the TensorFlow library (see https://www.tensorflow.org/guide).

- **PyTorch:** This is Facebook's contribution to production-worthy machine learning libraries. It is based on the Torch library, which makes use of GPUs in solving deep learning problems (see https://pytorch.org/docs/stable/index.html).

- **Scikit-learn:** This popular library for starting machine learning is built on top of NumPy and SciPy. It has classes for most of the traditional algorithms. You will learn more about Scikit-learn in the next section.

How Machine Learning Works

Machine learning algorithms can be divided into two types: unsupervised and supervised learning. Unsupervised learning involves discovering insights about data without preexisting results to test against. This generally means identifying patterns based on the data's characteristics without any input from a data scientist. Supervised learning involves using known data to train and test a model. Generally, the steps to training a supervised model are as follows:

1. Transform data.

2. Separate out test data.

3. Train the model.

4. Test accuracy.

Scikit-learn has tools to simplify each of these steps, as discussed in the following sections.

Transformations

For some algorithms, it is advantageous to transform the data before training a model. For example, you might want to turn a continuous variable, such as age, into discrete categories, such as age ranges. Scikit-learn includes many types of transformers, including transformers for cleaning, feature extraction, reduction, and expansion. These are represented as classes, which generally use a `.fit()` method to determine the transformation and a `.transform()` method to modify data using the transformation. Listing 11.1 uses the `MinMaxScaler` transformer, which scales values to fit in a defined range—between 0 and 1 by default.

Listing 11.1 **Transform Using MinMaxScaler**

```
import numpy as np
from sklearn.preprocessing import MinMaxScaler

data = np.array([[100, 34, 4],
                  90,  2,  0],
                  78, -12, 16],
                  23,  45, 4]]) # Array with data range -12 to 100

data
array([[100,  34,   4],
```

```
        [ 90,    2,    0],
        [ 78,  -12,   16],
        [ 23,   45,    4]])


minMax = MinMaxScaler()            # Create a transformer object
scaler = minMax.fit(data)          # Fit the transformer to the data

scaler.transform(data)             # Scale to range between 0 and 1
array([[1.       ,  0.80701754,  0.25      ],
       [0.87012987,  0.24561404,  0.       ],
       [0.71428571,  0.       ,  1.       ],
       [0.       ,  1.       ,  0.25      ]])
```

There may be times when you want to separate your data before fitting the transformer. When you do this, the transformer settings will not be affected by the test data. Fitting and transforming require separate methods; it is easy to fit to the train data and use that to transform the test data.

Splitting Test and Training Data

One important pitfall to avoid when training a model is overfitting, which occurs when a model perfectly predicts the data used to train it but has little predictive power with new data. In the simplest sense, you avoid overfitting by not testing the model with the data with which it was trained. Scikit-learn offers helper methods to make splitting data easy.

Before looking at an example of splitting data, you can load a simple example. Like a number of other data science libraries, Scikit-learn comes with some sample data sets. Listing 11.2 loads the iris data set. Notice that the .load_iris() functions loads two NumPy arrays of data: The first is the source data (the characteristics that will be used to make predictions), and the second is the target characteristic to predict. In the case of the iris data set, the source data has 150 samples of 4 characteristics and 150 targets that represent the types of iris.

Listing 11.2 **Loading a Sample Data Set**

```
from sklearn import datasets # Load the sample data sets
source, target = datasets.load_iris(return_X_y=True) # Load source and targets

print(type(source))
<class 'numpy.ndarray'>
print(source.shape)
(150, 4)

print(type(target))
<class 'numpy.ndarray'>
print(target.shape)
 (150,)
```

Listing 11.3 uses the Scikit-learn function `train_test_split()` to split the `iris` data set provided with the library into training and test data sets. You can see that the samples are split so that 112 of them are in the training set, and 38 of them are in the test set.

Listing 11.3   **Splitting a Data Set**

```
from sklearn.model_selection import train_test_split

train_s, test_s, train_t, test_t = train_test_split(source, target)
train_s.shape
(112, 4)

train_t.shape
(112,)

test_s.shape
(38, 4)

test_t.shape
(38,)
```

Training and Testing

Scikit-learn offers many classes representing various machine learning algorithms. These classes are referred to as *estimators*. Many estimators can be tuned using parameters during instantiation. Each estimator has a `.fit()` method, which trains the model. Most of the `.fit()` methods take two arguments. The first is some sort of training data, referred to as *samples*. The second is the results, or targets, for those samples. Both arguments should be array-like objects, such as NumPy arrays. When the training is done, the model can predict results by using its `.predict()` method. The accuracy of this prediction can be checked using functions from the method's module.

Listing 11.4 shows a simple example using the `KNeighborsClassifier` estimator. K-nearest neighbors is an algorithm that groups samples based on the distance between characteristics. It makes predictions by comparing a new sample to the existing samples that are its closest neighbors. You can tune the algorithm by choosing how many neighbors are compared to the new sample. When the model is trained, you can make predictions using the test data and check the accuracy of those predictions.

Listing 11.4   **Training a Model**

```
from sklearn.neighbors import KNeighborsClassifier    # Import estimator class
from sklearn import metrics    # Import the metrics module to test accuracy
knn = KNeighborsClassifier(n_neighbors=3)    # Create 3-neighbor estimator
knn.fit(train_s, train_t)    # Train the model using the training data
test_prediction = knn.predict(test_s)    # Make predictions from source data

metrics.accuracy_score(test_t, test_prediction)    # Accuracy against test data
0.8947368421052632
```

Learning More About Scikit-learn

This chapter only scratches the surface of Scikit-learn's capabilities. Other important features include tools for cross-validation, where a data set is split multiple times to avoid overfitting on test data, and pipelines, which wrap up transformers, estimators, and cross-validation together. If you want to learn more about Scikit-learn, you can find great tutorials at https://scikit-learn.org/stable/.

Summary

Many of the algorithms used to create machine learning models are represented in the major Python machine learning libraries. TensorFlow is a deep learning library created by Google. PyTorch is a library built on Torch by Facebook. Scikit-learn is a popular library for getting started with machine learning. It has modules and functions to perform the steps involved in creating and analyzing a model.

Questions

1. In which step of training a supervised estimator would a Scikit-learn transformer be useful?

2. Why is it important to separate training data and test data in machine learning?

3. After you have transformed your data and trained your model, what should you do next?

Natural Language Toolkit

One of the first things taught in introductory statistics textbooks is that correlation is not causation. It is also one of the first things forgotten.

Thomas Sowell

In This Chapter

- Introduction to the NLTK package
- Accessing and loading sample texts
- Using frequency distributions
- Text objects
- Classifying text

Using a computer to derive insights into text is incredibly useful. The subset of data science that addresses deriving insights into text is called *natural language processing*. The Natural Language Toolkit (NLTK) is a Python package for all things language processing. This chapter takes a quick look at this powerful package.

NLTK Sample Texts

The NLTK package offers sample texts from many sources that you can download and then use to explore language processing. Project Gutenberg is a project that puts copies of books online (see http://www.gutenberg.org). It is comprised largely of books in the public domain. A subset of this collection is available for download for use with NLTK. You can use the `nltk.download()` function to download the data into the nltk_data/corpora directory in your home directory:

```
import nltk
nltk.download('gutenberg')
[nltk_data] Downloading package gutenberg to
```

```
[nltk_data]      /Users/kbehrman/nltk_data...
[nltk_data]    Unzipping corpora/gutenberg.zip.
True
```

You can then import the data into your Python session as a corpus reader object:

> **Note**
>
> Each corpus reader is designed to read a specific collection of texts provided by NLTK.
>
> ```
> from nltk.corpus import gutenberg
> ```
>
> ```
> gutenberg
> ```
>
> ```
> <PlaintextCorpusReader in '/Users/kbehrman/nltk_data/corpora/gutenberg'>
> ```

There are corpus readers for different types of text sources. This example uses
PlaintextCorpusReader, which is designed for plaintext. You can list the individual texts by
using the fileids() method, which lists the filenames that can be used to load the texts:

```
gutenberg.fileids()
['austen-emma.txt',
 'austen-persuasion.txt',
 'austen-sense.txt',
 'bible-kjv.txt',
 'blake-poems.txt',
 'bryant-stories.txt',
 'burgess-busterbrown.txt',
 'carroll-alice.txt',
 'chesterton-ball.txt',
 'chesterton-brown.txt',
 'chesterton-thursday.txt',
 'edgeworth-parents.txt',
 'melville-moby_dick.txt',
 'milton-paradise.txt',
 'shakespeare-caesar.txt',
 'shakespeare-hamlet.txt',
 'shakespeare-macbeth.txt',
 'whitman-leaves.txt']
```

The corpus reader has different methods for reading the text. You can load the text broken into
individual words, sentences, or paragraphs. Listing 12.1 loads the text to William Shakespeare's
Julius Caesar in all three formats.

Listing 12.1 **Loading Text**

```
caesar_w = gutenberg.words('shakespeare-caesar.txt') # List of words
caesar_w
['[', 'The', 'Tragedie', 'of', 'Julius', 'Caesar', ...]
```

```
nltk.download('punkt') # Download tokenizer used to define sentence endings
[nltk_data] Downloading package punkt to /Users/kbehrman/nltk_data...
[nltk_data]   Unzipping tokenizers/punkt.zip.
True

caesar_s = gutenberg.sents('shakespeare-caesar.txt') # List of sentences
caesar_s
[['[', 'The', 'Tragedie', 'of', 'Julius', 'Caesar', 'by', 'William',
    'Shakespeare', '1599', ']'], ['Actus', 'Primus', '.'], ...]

caesar_p = gutenberg.paras('shakespeare-caesar.txt') # List of paragraphs
caesar_p
[[['[', 'The', 'Tragedie', 'of', 'Julius', 'Caesar', 'by', 'William', 'Shakespeare',
'1599', ']']], [['Actus', 'Primus', '.'], ['Scoena', 'Prima', '.']], ...]
```

Notice that before you can parse the text into sentences, you need to download the Punkt tokenizer. A *tokenizer* is used to break up, or tokenize, a piece of text. The Punkt tokenizer is used to break text into sentences. It is designed to work on texts of numerous languages.

Listing 12.2 shows how to look at the NLTK subdirectory of your home directory by using the shell command ls, which lists objects and directories. You can see that there are directories for corpora and tokenizers. In the corpora directory, you can see the downloaded collection. In the tokenizers directory, you can see the downloaded tokenizer. The punkt subdirectory contains files for each language covered.

Listing 12.2 **Data Directory**

```
!ls /root/nltk_data
corpora    tokenizers

!ls /root/nltk_data/corpora
gutenberg     gutenberg.zip

!ls /root/nltk_data/tokenizers
punkt    punkt.zip

!ls /root/nltk_data/tokenizers/punkt
PY3                english.pickle     greek.pickle       russian.pickle
README             estonian.pickle    italian.pickle     slovene.pickle
czech.pickle       finnish.pickle     norwegian.pickle   spanish.pickle
danish.pickle      french.pickle      polish.pickle      swedish.pickle
dutch.pickle       german.pickle      portuguese.pickle  turkish.pickle
```

Frequency Distributions

You can count the number of occurrences of each word in the text by using the nltk.FreqDist class. This class has methods that let you see which words appear most frequently and the number of distinct words a text contains. (In this case, the term *word* refers to any piece of text that is not white space.)

FreqDist separates punctuation as separate words from other text. The following example uses FreqDist to find the most common words in the text:

```
caesar_dist = nltk.FreqDist(caesar_w)
caesar_dist.most_common(15)
 [(',', 2204),
  ('.', 1296),
  ('I', 531),
  ('the', 502),
  (':', 499),
  ('and', 409),
  ("'", 384),
  ('to', 370),
  ('you', 342),
  ('of', 336),
  ('?', 296),
  ('not', 249),
  ('a', 240),
  ('is', 230),
  ('And', 218)]
```

If you want to see the most common words without including punctuation marks, you can filter out the punctuation. The Python Standard Library string module has a punctuation attribute that you can leverage for this purpose. Listing 12.3 loops through the original words of the text. It checks whether each item is a punctuation mark, and if it is not, it adds it to a new list in the variable caesar_r. This listing also compares the lengths of the original and the filtered file and finds 4,960 punctuation marks in the text. The listing then makes a new frequency distribution to show the most common non-punctuation words.

Listing 12.3 **Removing Punctuation**

```
import string
string.punctuation                       # Look at the punctuation string
'!"#$%&\'()*+,-./:;<=>?@[\\]^_'{|}~'


caesar_r = []
for word in caesar_w:
    if word not in string.punctuation:
        caesar_r.append(word)            # Add non-punctuation words


len(caesar_w) - len(caesar_r)            # Get number punctuation words
4960


caesar_dist = nltk.FreqDist(caesar_r)
caesar_dist.most_common(15)
[('I', 531),
 ('the', 502),
 ('and', 409),
 ('to', 370),
```

```
('you', 342),
('of', 336),
('not', 249),
('a', 240),
('is', 230),
('And', 218),
('d', 215),
('in', 204),
('that', 200),
('Caesar', 189),
('my', 188)]
```

You can see in Listing 12.3 that Caesar appears in the text 189 times. The other common words do not provide much insight into the text. You might want to filter out common words such as "the" and "is"; to do so, you use the NLTK corpus named stopwords. Listing 12.4 shows how to download this corpus and filter out these words before making a new frequency distribution.

Listing 12.4   **Filtering Stop Words**

```
nltk.download('stopwords')                    # Download stopwords corpus
from nltk.corpus import stopwords
[nltk_data] Downloading package stopwords to
[nltk_data]     /Users/kbehrman/nltk_data...
[nltk_data]     Unzipping corpora/stopwords.zip.

english_stopwords = stopwords.words('english')    # Load English stop words
english_stopwords[:10]
['i', 'me', 'my', 'myself', 'we', 'our', 'ours', 'ourselves', 'you', "you're"]

caesar_r = []
for word in caesar_w:
    if word not in string.punctuation:
        if word.lower() not in english_stopwords:
            caesar_r.append(word) # Not punctuation and not stop words

len(caesar_w) - len(caesar_r)
14706

caesar_dist = nltk.FreqDist(caesar_r)
caesar_dist.most_common(15)
[('Caesar', 189),
 ('Brutus', 161),
 ('Bru', 153),
 ('haue', 128),
 ('shall', 107),
 ('Cassi', 107),
 ('thou', 100),
 ('Cassius', 85),
 ('Antony', 75),
 ('know', 66),
```

```
('Enter', 63),
('men', 62),
('vs', 62),
('man', 58),
('thee', 55)]
```

The list of the most common words now gives you more insight into the text: You can see which characters are mentioned the most. Not surprisingly, Caesar and Brutus are at the top of the list.

Listing 12.5 looks at some of the methods of the `FreqDist` class.

Listing 12.5   **The FreqDist Class**

```
caesar_dist.max()                  # Get the word with the most appearances
'Caesar'

caesar_dist['Cassi']     # Get the count for a particular word
107

caesar_dist.freq('Cassi') # Count of the word divided by total  count
0.009616248764267098

caesar_dist.N()            # Get number of words
11127

caesar_dist.tabulate(10)  # Display the counts for the top 10 words
Caesar   Brutus     Bru    haue   shall   Cassi    thou Cassius  Antony    know
  189      161       153    128     107     107      100     85      75      66
```

`FreqDist` also comes with a built-in plot method. The following example plots the 10 most frequently appearing words (see Figure 12.1):

```
caesar_dist.plot(10)
```

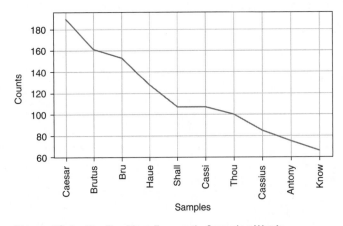

Figure 12.1   The Ten Most Frequently Occurring Words

Text Objects

The NLTK library offers a Text class that provides functionality that is useful when you are beginning to explore a new text. The Text class takes a list of words as an argument during initialization:

```
from nltk.text import Text
caesar_t = Text(caesar_w)
type(caesar_t)
nltk.text.Text
```

The Text.concordance() method shows the context around a given word. In this example, it shows five examples of Antony in context:

```
caesar_t.concordance('Antony', lines=5)
Displaying  5 of 75 matches:
efulnesse . Exeunt . Enter Caesar , Antony for the Course , Calphurnia , Porti
 Of that quicke Spirit that is in Antony : Let me not hinder Cassius your de
He loues no Playes , As thou dost Antony : he heares no Musicke ; Seldome he
r ' d him the Crowne ? Cask . Why Antony Bru . Tell vs the manner of it , ge
I did not marke it . I sawe Marke Antony offer him a Crowne , yet ' twas not
```

The Text.collocations() method displays words that most commonly appear together:

```
caesar_t.collocations(num=4)
Mark Antony; Marke Antony; Good morrow; Caius Ligarius
```

The Text.similar() method finds words that appear in contexts similar to a given word:

```
caesar_t.similar('Caesar')
me it brutus you he rome that cassius this if men worke him vs feare world thee
```

The Text.findall() method prints text that matches a regular expression to search text. You can define the regular expression match pattern by using < and > to define word boundaries and .* as a wildcard that matches anything. The following pattern then matches all occurrences of the word O followed by any word that starts with C:

```
caesar_t.findall(r'<O><C.*>')
O Cicero; O Cassius; O Conspiracie; O Caesar; O Caesar; O Caesar; O
Constancie; O Caesar; O Caesar; O Caesar; O Cassius; O Cassius; O
Cassius; O Coward; O Cassius; O Clitus
```

The Text.dispersion_plot() method lets you compare where in a text given words occur (see Figure 12.2):

```
caesar_t.dispersion_plot(['Caesar', 'Antony', 'Brutus', 'Cassi'])
```

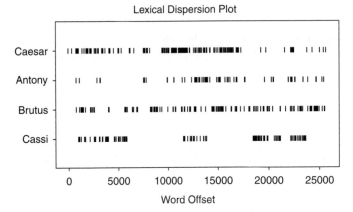

Figure 12.2   Results of the Text.dispersion_plot() Method

Classifying Text

NLTK has classifier classes that implement different algorithms for handling the labeling of text data. Generally, to create a model for classifying text, you need to prepare a set of features paired with a category or label. This section walks through a simple example using the Brown corpus that is available through NLTK (see http://korpus.uib.no/icame/brown/bcm.html). This corpus has precategorized texts.

Say that you believe you can label a paragraph from one of these texts as either editorial or fiction, based on the appearance of certain words, pointed to by the variable tell_words:

```
tell_words = ['american', 'city', 'congress', 'country', 'county',
              'editor', 'fact', 'government', 'national', 'nuclear',
              'party', 'peace', 'political', 'power', 'president',
              'public', 'state', 'states', 'united', 'war',
              'washington', 'world', 'big', 'church', 'every', 'eyes',
              'face', 'felt', 'found', 'god', 'hand', 'head', 'home',
              'house', 'knew', 'moment', 'night', 'room', 'seemed',
              'stood', 'think', 'though', 'thought', 'told', 'voice']
```

Listing 12.6 shows how to download the corpuses you will use and get paragraphs for the editorial and fiction categories.

Listing 12.6   **Downloading Corpuses**

```
nltk.download('brown')                          # Download the Brown corpus
[nltk_data] Downloading package brown to /Users/kbehrman/nltk_data...
[nltk_data]   Unzipping corpora/brown.zip.

from nltk.corpus import brown
nltk.download('stopwords')
from nltk.corpus import stopwords
english_stopwords = stopwords.words('english')
```

```
ed_p = brown.paras(categories='editorial') # Load only editorial paragraphs

fic_p = brown.paras(categories='fiction')  # Load only fiction paragraphs

print(len(ed_p))
1003

print(len(fic_p))
1043
```

The format of the supplied paragraphs is lists of lists, with the sublists representing sentences. For the purpose of this exercise, say that you want a set of words for each paragraph. Listing 12.7 defines a flattening method and then flattens the paragraphs in each data set.

Listing 12.7 **Flattening Nested Lists**

```
def flatten(paragraph):
    output = set([])                        # Use a set as you only care about a
single occurrence of a word
    for item in paragraph:
        if isinstance(item, (list, tuple)): # Add item is a list or tuple
            output.update(item)
        else:
            output.add(item)                # Add item
    return output

ed_flat = []
for paragraph in ed_p:
    ed_flat.append(flatten(paragraph))       # Flatten the editorial paragraphs
fic_flat = []
for paragraph in fic_p:
    fic_flat.append(flatten(paragraph))      # Flatten the fiction paragraphs
```

Next, you need to pair each paragraph with the label based on its source category. Listing 12.8 does this for both editorial and fiction texts and then shuffles the order, using the shuffle method from the random module, to ensure that the order will not influence the classifier.

Listing 12.8 **Labeling Data**

```
labeled_data = []
for paragraph in ed_flat:
    labeled_data.append((paragraph, 'editorial'))

for paragraph in fic_flat:
    labeled_data.append((paragraph, 'fiction'))

from random import shuffle
shuffle(labeled_data)
```

The classifier does not use the original paragraphs but rather expects a feature set. This feature set will be in the form of a dictionary that maps features to values. Listing 12.9 defines a function to create a feature dictionary whose values are set to True if a tell word is found in the paragraph and False if not. It then uses this to list paired features and labels. It splits this information into training and test data so you can train your classifier.

Listing 12.9   **Defining Features**

```
def define_features(paragraph):
    features = {}
    for tell_word in tell_words:
        features[tell_word] = tell_word in paragraph
    return features


feature_data = []
for labeled_paragraph in labeled_data:
    paragraph, label = labeled_paragraph
    feature_data.append((define_features(paragraph), label,))


train_data = feature_data[:1400]
test_data = feature_data[1400:]
```

Listing 12.10 shows how to train the model, using the nltk.NaiveBayesClassifier class, and use the trained model to classify an individual feature set, check which of the tell words had the most influence on the training, and then check the accuracy by using the test data.

Listing 12.10   **Training and Testing the Model**

```
bayes = nltk.NaiveBayesClassifier.train(train_data) # Train a model
bayes.classify(train_data[0][0]) # Classify one of the training set paragraphs
'fictio'


bayes.show_most_informative_features()
Most Informative Features
                knew = True           fictio : editor =     22.3 : 1.0
              editor = True           editor : fictio =     16.6 : 1.0
               stood = True           fictio : editor =     16.0 : 1.0
           political = True           editor : fictio =     14.5 : 1.0
             nuclear = True           editor : fictio =     12.4 : 1.0
          government = True           editor : fictio =     10.8 : 1.0
             thought = True           fictio : editor =     10.2 : 1.0
              seemed = True           fictio : editor =      7.0 : 1.0
            national = True           editor : fictio =      6.6 : 1.0
              public = True           editor : fictio =      6.5 : 1.0


nltk.classify.accuracy(bayes, test_data) # Check the accuracy
0.6842105263157895
```

You can see that the model is about 66% accurate in predicting the labels for the test data; this is better than a coin flip.

This example should give you a sense of using an NLTK classifier. There is much more to NLTK than you have learned about in this chapter. If you want to learn more about natural language processing using NLTK, check out the book *Natural Language Processing with Python*, authored by the creators of the library (see http://www.nltk.org/book).

Summary

The library NLTK contains tools for processing text and comes with sample texts that you can download and work with. The `FreqDist` class lets you gain insights into the frequency at which different words appear. The `Text` class provides a handy way to explore a new text. NLTK comes with built-in classifier classes that can be used to categorize text based on training data.

Exercises

1. Load the text *Emma* by Jane Austen as words, sentences, and paragraphs.

2. Count the occurrence of the word Alice in *Alice in Wonderland* by Lewis Carroll.

3. Use `tabulate` to view the top 10 words in *Alice in Wonderland*, excluding punctuation and stop words.

4. Find words that are similar to rabbit in *Alice in Wonderland*.

5. Use the corpus `names` to find the 10 most frequently occurring names in *Hamlet*.

Part III

Intermediate Python

Functional Programming

Controlling complexity is the essence of computer programming.

Brian Kernighan

In This Chapter

- Introduction to functional programming
- State and scope
- Functional functions
- List comprehensions
- Generators

As you have seen so far in this book, a Python program, at its most basic, is composed of a series of statements, which can be simple or compound. The way in which you organize these statements has ramifications for performance, readability, and ease of modification. Some approaches that have been widely adopted are procedural programming, functional programming, and object-oriented programming. This chapter introduces some of the concepts of functional programming, including comprehensions and generators, both of which were borrowed from purely functional languages.

Introduction to Functional Programming

Functional programming is based on the mathematical definition of functions. A function, in this sense, maps an input to an output. For any input, there can only be a single output; in other words, the output for a distinct input will always be the same. Some programming languages, such as Haskell and Erlang, adhere to this limitation strictly. Python is flexible enough that it can adopt some functional concepts without the strictness. Functional programming in Python is sometimes referred to as *functional light programming*.

Scope and State

The *state* of a program comprises names, definitions, and values that exist at a certain time in that program, including function definitions, modules imported, and values assigned to variables. State has what's known as a *scope*—the area of the program for which the state holds. Scopes are hierarchical. When you indent a block of code, this code has a nested scope. It inherits scope from the unindented code around it but does not directly change the outer scope.

Listing 13.1 sets values for the variables a and b in the outer scope. Then the code block of the function sets a to a different value and prints both variables. You can see that when the function is called, it uses its own definition of the variable a but inherits that definition for b from the outer scope. In the outer scope, the value assigned by the function to a is ignored, as it is out of scope.

Listing 13.1   **Inheriting Scope**

```
a = 'a outer'
b = 'b outer'

def scoped_function():
    a = 'a inner'
    print(a)
    print(b)

scoped_function()
a inner
b outer

print(a)
a outer

print(b)
b outer
```

Depending on Global State

The code in this book up until now has mostly been presented using the procedural approach. In this approach, the current state is defined by the statements that have run on the lines before the present one. This state is shared through the program and modified throughout. This means that a function that uses the state to determine its output could have a different output with the same input. Let's look at some examples contrasting the procedural approach with a functional one.

Listing 13.2 creates a function, describe_the_wind(), which returns a sentence using a variable, wind, defined in the outer scope. You can see that the output of this function will be different depending on this variable.

Listing 13.2   **Depending on Outer Scope**

```
wind = 'Southeast'

def describe_the_wind():
    return f'The wind blows from the {wind}'

describe_the_wind()
'The wind blows from the Southeast'

wind = 'North'
describe_the_wind()
'The wind blows from the North'        f
```

A more functional approach is to pass the variable as an argument. In this way, the function will return the same value for a value passed to it, regardless of the outer state:

```
def describe_the_wind(wind):
    return f'The wind blows from the {wind}'

describe_the_wind('Northeast')
'The wind blows from the Northeast'
```

Changing State

In addition to not relying on outside state, a functional function should not directly change outside state. Listing 13.3 shows a program that changes an outer state variable, WIND, within the function change_wind(). Notice the use of the keyword global, which indicates to change an outer state variable rather than define a new variable in the inner state.

Listing 13.3   **Modifying Outer Scope**

```
WINDS = ['Northeast', 'Northwest', 'Southeast', 'Southwest']
WIND = WINDS[0]

def change_wind():
    global WIND
    WIND = WINDS[(WINDS.index(WIND) + 1)%3]

WIND
'Northeast'

change_wind()
WIND
'Northwest'
```

```
for _ in WINDS:
    print(WIND)
    change_wind()
Northwest
Southeast
Northeast
Northwest
```

A more functional approach to getting the same output is to move the winds variable into the inner state and have the function change_wind() take an argument to determine the output, as shown in Listing 13.4.

Listing 13.4   **Not Modifying Outer Scope**

```
def change_wind(wind_index):
    winds = ['Northeast', 'Northwest', 'Southeast', 'Southwest']
    return winds[wind_index]

print( change_wind(0) )
Northeast

print( change_wind(1) )
Northwest

print( change_wind(2) )
Southeast

print( change_wind(3) )
Southwest
```

Changing Mutable Data

A more subtle way of changing outside state is by passing mutable objects. Remember that mutable objects are objects, such as lists and dictionaries, whose contents can be changed. If you set a variable in an outer state, pass it as an argument to a function, and then change its value in the function's inner state, the outer state version of the variable will retain its original value. Here is an example:

```
b = 1

def foo(a):
    a = 2

foo(b)
print(b)
1
```

However, if you pass a mutable object, such as a dictionary, as an argument to a function, any change made to that object in the function will be reflected in the outer state as well. The following example defines a function that takes a dictionary as an argument and changes one of its values:

```
d = {"vehicle": "ship", "owner": "Joseph Bruce Ismay"}
```

```
def change_mutable_data(data):
    '''A function which changes mutable data.'''
    data['owner'] = 'White Star Line'
```

```
change_mutable_data(d)
print(d)
{'vehicle': 'ship', 'owner': 'White Star Line'}
```

You can see that the dictionary, d, when passed to this function, had its value changed in the outer state.

Changing the outside scope of mutable objects in this manner can lead to subtle bugs. One way to avoid this, if your data structure isn't too big, is to make a copy in the inner scope, and manipulate the copy:

```
d = {"vehicle": "ship", "owner": "Joseph Bruce Ismay"}
```

```
def change_owner(data):
    new_data = data.copy()
    new_data['owner'] = 'White Star Line'
    return new_data
```

```
changed = change_owner(d)
changed
{'owner': 'White Star Line', 'vehicle': 'ship'}
```

By working on the copy, it is much easier to see where the values are changed.

Functional Programming Functions

Three built-in Python functions that come from the functional programming world are map(), filter(), and reduce().

The map() function applies to a sequence of values and returns a map object. The input sequence can be any iterable type—that is, any object that can be iterated, such as a Python sequence. The map object returned is an iterable also, so you can loop through it or cast it to a list to view the results:

```
def grow_flowers(d):
    return d * "❀"
```

```
gardens = map(grow_flowers, [0,1,2,3,4,5])
```

```
type(gardens)
map
```

```
list(gardens)
['', '🌸', '🌸🌸', '🌸🌸🌸', '🌸🌸🌸🌸', '🌸🌸🌸🌸🌸']
```

You can supply map() with a function that takes multiple arguments and supply multiple sequences of input values:

```
l1 = [0,1,2,3,4]
l2 = [11,10,9,8,7,6]
```

```
def multi(d1, d2):
    return d1 * d2
```

```
result = map(multi, l1, l2)
print( list(result) )
 [0, 10, 18, 24, 28]
```

Notice in this example that one of the input sequences is longer than the other. The map() function stops when it reaches the end of the shortest input sequence.

The reduce() function also takes a function and an iterable as arguments. It then uses the function to return a single value, based on the input. For example, if you want to subtract an amount from an account balance, you can do it with a for loop, like this:

```
initial_balance = 10000
debits = [20, 40, 300, 3000, 1, 234]
```

```
balance = initial_balance
```

```
for debit in debits:
    balance -= debit
```

```
balance
6405
```

You could achieve the same result by using the reduce() function, like this:

```
from functools import reduce
```

```
inital_balance = 10000
debits = [20, 40, 300, 3000, 1, 234]
```

```
def minus(a, b):
    return a - b
```

```
balance = reduce(minus, debits, initial_balance)
balance
6405
```

The operator module provides all the standard operators as functions, including functions for the standard mathematical operations. You can use the operator.sub() function as an argument to reduce() as a replacement for the minus() function:

```
from functools import reduce
import operator

initial_balance = 10000
debits = [20, 40, 300, 3000, 1, 234]

reduce(operator.sub, debits, initial_balance)
6405
```

The filter() function takes a function and an iterable as arguments. The function should return True or False, based on each item. The result is an iterable object of only input values that causes the function to return True. For example, to get only the capital letters from a string, you can define a function that tests whether a character is capitalized and pass it and the string to filter():

```
charles = 'ChArlesTheBald'

def is_cap(a):
    return a.isupper()

retval = filter(is_cap, charles)
list(retval)
['C', 'A', 'T', 'B']
```

One of the few times I really recommend using lambda functions is when you're using the map(), filter(), and reduce() functions. When you are doing a simple comparison—such as for all the numbers less than 10 and greater than 3—you can use a lambda function and range() in a clean and easy-to-read way:

```
nums = filter(lambda x: x > 3, range(10))
list(nums)
 [4, 5, 6, 7, 8, 9]
```

List Comprehensions

List comprehensions are syntax borrowed from the functional programming language Haskell (see https://docs.python.org/3/howto/functional.html). Haskell is a fully functional programming language implemented with syntax that lends itself to a purely functional approach. You can think of a list comprehension as a one-line for loop that returns a list. Although the source of list comprehensions is in functional programming, their use has become standard in all Python approaches.

List Comprehension Basic Syntax

The basic syntax for a list comprehension is as follows:

```
[ \<item returned\> for \<source item\> in \<iterable\> ]
```

For example, given a list of names for which you want to change the names to title capitalization (so that the first letter is uppercase), you use x.title() as the item returned and each name as a source item:

```
names = ['tim', 'tiger', 'tabassum', 'theodora', 'tanya']
capd = [x.title() for x in names]
capd
['Tim', 'Tiger', 'Tabassum', 'Theodora', 'Tanya']
```

This would be the equivalent process using a for loop:

```
names = ['tim', 'tiger', 'tabassum', 'theodora', 'tanya']
capd = []

for name in names:
    capd.append(name.title())


capd
['Tim', 'Tiger', 'Tabassum', 'Theodora', 'Tanya']
```

Replacing map and filter

You can use list comprehensions as replacements for the map() and filter() functions. For example, the following code maps the numbers 0 through 5, with a function that inserts them into a string:

```
def count_flower_petals(d):
    return f"{d} petals counted so far"


counts = map(count_flower_petals, range(6))


list(counts)
['0 petals counted so far',
 '1 petals counted so far',
 '2 petals counted so far',
 '3 petals counted so far',
 '4 petals counted so far',
 '5 petals counted so far']
```

You can replace this code with the following much simpler list comprehension:

```
[f"{x} petals counted so far" for x in range(6)]
['0 petals counted so far',
 '1 petals counted so far',
 '2 petals counted so far',
 '3 petals counted so far',
 '4 petals counted so far',
 '5 petals counted so far']
```

You can also add a conditional to a list comprehension, using the following syntax:

```
[ \<item returned\> for \<source item\> in \<iterable\> if \<condition\> ]
```

By using a conditional, you can easily duplicate the functionality of the filter() function. For instance, the following filter() example returns only uppercase letters:

```
characters = ['C', 'b', 'c', 'A', 'b', 'P', 'g', 'S']
def cap(a):
    return a.isupper()

retval = filter(cap, characters)

list(retval)
['C', 'A', 'P', 'S']
```

You can replace this function with the following list comprehension that uses a conditional:

```
characters = ['C', 'b', 'c', 'A', 'b','P', 'g', 'S']
[x for x in characters if x.isupper()]
['C', 'A', 'P', 'S']
```

Multiple Variables

If the items in a source iterable are sequences, you can unpack them by using multiple variables:

```
points = [(12, 3), (-1, 33), (12, 0)]

[ f'x: {x} y: {y}' for x, y in points ]
['x: 12 y: 3', 'x: -1 y: 33', 'x: 12 y: 0']
```

You can perform the equivalent of nested for loops by using multiple for statements in the same list comprehensions:

```
list_of_lists = [[1,2,3], [4,5,6], [7,8,9]]

[x for y in list_of_lists for x in y]
[1, 2, 3, 4, 5, 6, 7, 8, 9]
```

Dictionary Comprehensions

Dictionary comprehensions use a syntax similar to that of list comprehensions. However, whereas you append a single value to a list, you add a key/value pair to a dictionary. This example uses the values in two lists to construct a dictionary:

```
names = ['James', 'Jokubus', 'Shaemus']
scores = [12, 33, 23]

{ name:score for name in names for score in scores}
{'James': 23, 'Jokubus': 23, 'Shaemus': 23}
```

Generators

One of the big advantages of using a range object over using a list when dealing with big numeric ranges is that the range object calculates results as you request them. This means that its memory footprint is consistently small. Generators let you use your own calculations to create values on demand, working in a similar way to range objects.

Generator Expressions

One way to create generators is through generator expressions, which use the same syntax as list comprehensions except that the enclosing square brackets are replaced with parentheses. This example shows how to create a list and a generator based on the same calculation and print them:

```
l_ten = [x**3 for x in range(10)]
g_ten = (x**3 for x in range(10))

print(f"l_ten is a {type(l_ten)}")
l_ten is a <class 'list'>


print(f"l_ten prints as: {l_ten}")
l_ten prints as: [0, 1, 8, 27, 64, 125, 216, 343, 512, 729]

print(f"g_ten is a {type(g_ten)}")
g_ten is a <class 'generator'>

print(f"g_ten prints as: {g_ten}")
g_ten prints as: <generator object <genexpr> at 0x7f3704d52f68>
```

When you print the list, you can see its contents; this is not the case with the generator. To get a value from a generator, you have to request the next value, which you can do by using the next() function:

```
next(g_ten)
0
```

Or, more commonly, you can iterate through a generator in a for loop:

```
for x in g_ten:
    print(x)
1
8
27
64
125
216
343
512
729
```

Because generators only generate values on demand, there is no way to index or slice them:

```
g_ten[3]
```
```
--------------------------------------------------------------------------
TypeError                          Traceback (most recent call last)
<ipython-input-6-e7b8f961aa33> in <module>()
      1
----> 2 g_ten[3]

TypeError: 'generator' object is not subscriptable
```

One of the important advantages of generators over lists is their memory footprint. The following examples use the sys.getsizeof() function to compare the sizes of a list and a generator:

```
import sys
x = 100000000
l_big = [x for x in range(x)]
g_big = (x for x in range(x))

print( f"l_big is {sys.getsizeof(l_big)} bytes")
l_big is 859724472 bytes

print( f"g_big is {sys.getsizeof(g_big)} bytes")
g_big is 88 bytes
```

Generator Functions

You can use generator functions to create complex generators. Generator functions look like normal functions but with the return statement replaced with a yield statement. The generator keeps its own internal state, returning values as requested:

```
def square_them(numbers):
    for number in numbers:
        yield number * number


s = square_them(range(10000))

print(next(s))
0

print(next(s))
1

print(next(s))
4

print(next(s))
9
```

An additional advantage of generators over lists is the ability to create an infinite generator—that is, a generator with no end. An infinite generator returns as many values as requested. For example, you can make a generator that increments a number as many times as you like:

```
def counter(d):
    while True:
        d += 1
        yield d


c = counter(10)

print(next(c))
11

print(next(c))
12

print(next(c))
13
```

Listing 13.5 chains together four generators. This is a useful way to keep each generator understandable, while still harnessing the just-in-time calculations of the generators.

Listing 13.5 **Generator Pipeline**

```
evens = (x*2 for x in range(5000000))
three_factors = (x//3 for x in evens if x%3 == 0)
titles = (f"this number is {x}" for x in three_factors)
capped = (x.title() for x in titles)

print(f"The first call to capped: {next(capped)}")
The first call to capped: This Number Is 0

print(f"The second call to capped: {next(capped)}") The second call to capped: This
Number Is 2

print(f"The third call to capped: {next(capped)}")
The third call to capped: This Number Is 4
```

Using generators is a great way to make your code performant. You should consider using them whenever you are iterating through a long sequence of calculated values.

Summary

Functional programming is an approach to organizing programs that is useful for designing software that can be run concurrently. It is based on the idea that a function's inner state should be changed by or should change the outer state of the code calling it. A function should always return the same value for a given input. Three built-in Python functions that come from the functional programming world are map(), filter(), and reduce(). Using list comprehensions and generators are both very Pythonic ways of creating sequences of values. Using generators is recommended when you're iterating through any large number of values or when you don't know how many values you need.

Questions

1. What would the following code print?

```
a = 1
b = 2

def do_something(c):
    c = 3
    a = 4
    print(a)
    return c

b = do_something(b)
print(a + b)
```

2. Use the map() function to take the string 'omni' and return the list ['oo','mm', 'nn', 'ii'].

3. Use the sum() function, which sums the contents of a sequence, with a list comprehension to find the summation of the positive even numbers below 100.

4. Write a generator expression that returns cubed numbers up to 1,000.

5. A Fibonacci sequence starts with 0 and 1, and every subsequent number is the sum of the previous two numbers. Write a generator function that calculates a Fibonacci sequence.

Object-Oriented Programming

Any fool can write code that a computer can understand.
Good programmers write code that humans can understand.

Martin Fowler

In This Chapter

- Linking state and function
- Classes and objects
- Special functions
- Class inheritance

The object-oriented approach to programming is one of the most popular approaches. It is an approach that tries to model objects and their relationships by combining functionality and data. If you think of modeling a car in code, the object-oriented approach is to have both methods that take actions such as accelerating or breaking as well as data such as the amount of fuel in the gas tank attached to the same object. Other approaches would keep the data (the gas level, in this case) separate from the function definitions, perhaps passing the data as arguments to the functions. The big advantage of the object-oriented approach is the ability to make human-understandable representations of complex systems.

Grouping State and Function

Unlike the functional approach, object-oriented programming bundles data and functionality together into bundles known as *objects*. It can be argued that everything in Python is an object; even basic types have methods as well as data. For example, an int object doesn't just hold a value; it also has methods. One of these methods is the to_bytes() method, which converts values to their bytes representations:

```
my_num = 13
my_num.to_bytes(8, 'little')
b'\r\x00\x00\x00\x00\x00\x00'
```

More complex data types, such as lists, strings, dictionaries, and Pandas DataFrames, all combine data and functionality. In Python, a function that is attached to an object is referred to as a *method*. The power in Python's object-oriented capabilities is that you can use objects from provided libraries, and you can also design your own objects.

Classes and Instances

Objects are defined by classes. Think of a class as a template for an object. When you instantiate a class, you get an object of that class type. The syntax for creating a basic class definition is as follows:

```
class <class name>():
    <statement>
```

You can use a pass statement to define a simple class that does nothing:

```
class DoNothing():
    pass
```

The syntax for instantiating a class is as follows:

```
<class name>()
```

So, to create an instance named do_nothing from the DoNothing class, you would instantiate the object like this:

```
do_nothing = DoNothing()
```

If you check the type of this object:

```
type(do_nothing)
__main__.DoNothing
```

you see that it is a new type, defined by the DoNothing class. You can confirm this by using the built-in isinstance() function, which tests if an object is an instance of a particular class:

```
isinstance(do_nothing, DoNothing)
True
```

The most common way to define a method attached to a class is to indent the function definition to the inner scope of the class, using this syntax:

```
class <CLASS NAME>():
    def <FUNCTION NAME>():
        <STATEMENT>
```

The first argument to the function is the instance from which it is called. By convention, this is named self. The following example defines a class, DoSomething, with the method return_self(), which returns self, and then makes an instance and demonstrates that the return value of return_self() is in fact the instance itself:

```
class DoSomething():
    def return_self(self):
        return self


do_something = DoSomething()


do_something == do_something.return_self()
True
```

> **Note**
>
> Although you are required to have self as a parameter in the method definition, when you call the method, you don't specify self, as it is passed automatically behind the scenes.

Outside of the self parameter, you can define methods just as you would other functions. You can also use the self object to create and access object variables within the class definition by using this syntax:

```
self.<VARIABLE NAME>
```

In a similar way, methods and attributes will be attached to the object instantiated from the class:

```
class AddAttribute():
    def add_score(self):
        self.score = 14


add_attribute = AddAttribute()
add_attribute.add_score()


add_attribute.score
14
```

To call one method from another in the same class, you use the following syntax:

```
self.<METHOD NAME>
```

Listing 14.1 demonstrates how to call one method from another in the same class.

Listing 14.1   **Calling Methods Internally**

```
class InternalMethodCaller():
    def method_one(self):
        print('Calling method one')

    def method_two(self, n):
        print(f'Method two calling method one {n} times')
        for _ in range(n):
            self.method_one()
```

```
internal_method_caller = InternalMethodCaller()
internal_method_caller.method_one()
Calling method one

internal_method_caller.method_two(2)
Method two calling method one   2 times
Calling method one
Calling method one
```

Private Methods and Variables

The methods and variables of an object are accessible to anyone who has access to that object. The methods and variables you have seen so far are known as *public* because they represent data and functionality that are meant to be used directly. Sometimes in the process of defining a class, you need to define variables or methods that you do not want to be used directly. These are known as *private* attributes, and their implementation details could change as a class evolves. Private attributes are used by public methods internally. Python does not have a mechanism to prevent access to private attributes, but a private attribute's name typically begins with an underscore, as shown in the following example:

```
class PrivatePublic():
    def _private_method(self):
        print('private')

    def public_method(self):
        # Call private
        self._private_method()
        # ... Do something else
```

Class Variables

Variables you define by using the syntax self.<VARIABLE NAME> are known as *instance variables*. These variables are bound to the individual instances of a class. Each instance can have a different value for its instance variables. You can also bind variables to a class. These *class variables* are shared by all instances of that class. Listing 14.2 demonstrates a class with both a class variable and an instance variable. The two instances of this class share the data of the class variable, but have unique values for the instance variable. Notice that the class variable is not attached to the instance object, self.

Listing 14.2 **Class and Instance Variables**

```
class ClassyVariables():
    class_variable = 'Yellow'

    def __init__(self, color):
        self.instance_variable = color
```

```
red = ClassyVariables('Red')
blue = ClassyVariables('Blue')

red.instance_variable
'Red'

red.class_variable
'Yellow'

blue.class_variable
'Yellow'

blue.instance_variable
'Blue'
```

Special Methods

In Python, some special method names are reserved for certain functionality. These include methods for operator and container functionality as well as object initialization. The most frequently used of these methods is the __init__() method, which is called every time an object is instantiated. It is generally used to set up initial attribute values for an object. Listing 14.3 defines a class, Initialized, with an __init__() method, which takes an extra parameter, n. When you instantiate an instance of this class, you must supply a value for this parameter, and it is then assigned to the variable count. This variable can then be accessed by other methods in the class as self.count or from the instantiated object as <object>.<attribute>.

Listing 14.3   The __init__ Method

```
class Initialized():
    def __init__(self, n):
        self.count = n

    def increment_count(self):
        self.count += 1

initialized = Initialized(2)
initialized.count
2

initialized.increment_count()
initialized.count
3
```

Representation Methods

The methods __repr__() and __str__() are used to control how an object is represented. The __repr__() method is meant to give a technical description of an object. Ideally this description includes the information necessary to re-create the object. This is the representation you see if you use an object as a statement. The __str__() method is meant to define a less strict but more human-friendly representation. This is the output when you cast an object to a string, as is done automatically by the print() function. Listing 14.4 shows both __repr__() and __str__() in use.

Listing 14.4   __repr__ and __str__

```
class Represented():
    def __init__(self, n):
        self.n = n

    def __repr__(self):
        return f'Represented({self.n})'

    def __str__(self):
        return 'Object demonstrating __str__ and __repr__'

represented = Represented(13)

represented
Represented(13)

r = eval(represented.__repr__())
type(r)
__main__.Represented

r.n
13

str(represented)
'Object demonstrating __str__ and __repr__'

print(represented)
Object demonstrating __str__ and __repr__
```

Rich Comparison Methods

Rich comparison methods are used to define how an object will behave when used with Python's built-in operators. Listing 14.5 shows how to define methods for the various comparison operators. The CompareMe class uses the variable score to determine comparisons, and it falls back to the variable time only when necessary.

Listing 14.5 **Comparison Methods**

```
class CompareMe():
    def __init__(self, score, time):
        self.score = score
        self.time = time

    def __lt__(self, O):
        """ Less than"""
        print('called __lt__')
        if self.score == O.score:
            return self.time > O.time
        return self.score < O.score

    def __le__(self, O):
        """Less than or equal"""
        print('called __le__')
        return self.score <= O.score

    def __eq__(self, O):
        """Equal"""
        print('called __eq__')
        return (self.score, self.time) == (O.score, O.time)

    def __ne__(self, O):
        """Not Equal"""
        print('called __ne__')
        return (self.score, self.time) != (O.score, O.time)

    def __gt__(self, O):
        """Greater Than"""
        print('called __gt__')
        if self.score == O.score:
            return self.time < O.time
        return self.score > O.score

    def __ge__(self, O):
        """Greater Than or Equal"""
        print('called __ge__')
        return self.score >= O.score
```

Listing 14.6 instantiates the CompareMe class with some different values and then tests some of
the comparison operators.

Listing 14.6 **Trying Operators**

```
high_score  = CompareMe(100, 100)
mid_score   = CompareMe(50, 50)
mid_score_1 = CompareMe(50, 50)
low_time    = CompareMe(100, 25)
```

```
high_score > mid_score
called __gt__
True

high_score >= mid_score_1
called __ge__
True

high_score == low_time
called __eq__
False

mid_score == mid_score_1
called __eq__
True

low_time > high_score
called __gt__
True
```

It is possible to define comparisons that compare an attribute to an object. Listing 14.7 creates a class that directly compares its score attribute to another object. This lets you compare an object to any other type that is comparable to an int. (For the sake of brevity, this listing implements only the less-than and equals methods.)

Listing 14.7   **Comparing to an Object**

```
class ScoreMatters():
    def __init__(self, score):
        self.score = score

    def __lt__(self, 0):
        return self.score < 0

    def __eq__(self, 0):
        return self.score == 0

my_score = ScoreMatters(14)
my_score == 14.0
True

my_score < 15
True
```

It is important not to define confusing or illogical comparisons in Python code. You need to keep the end user in mind in these definitions. For example, Listing 14.8 defines a class that is always bigger than anything it is compared to—even itself. This would probably lead to confusion for an end user of the class.

Listing 14.8   **A Confusingly Big Class**

```
class ImAllwaysBigger():
    def __gt__(self, 0):
        return True

    def __ge__(self, 0):
        return True

i_am_bigger = ImAllwaysBigger()
no_i_am_bigger = ImAllwaysBigger()

i_am_bigger > "Anything"
True

i_am_bigger > no_i_am_bigger
True

no_i_am_bigger > i_am_bigger
True

i_am_bigger > i_am_bigger
True
```

Math Operator Methods

There are special Python methods for math operations. Listing 14.9 defines a class that implements methods for the +, -, and * operators. This class returns new objects based on its .value variable.

Listing 14.9   **Selected Math Operations**

```
class MathMe():
    def __init__(self, value):
        self.value = value

    def __add__(self, 0):
        return MathMe(self.value + 0.value)

    def __sub__(self, 0):
        return MathMe(self.value - 0.value)

    def __mul__(self, 0):
        return MathMe(self.value * 0.value)

m1 = MathMe(3)
m2 = MathMe(4)
m3 = m1 + m2
```

```
m3.value
7

m4 = m1 - m3
m4.value
-4

m5 = m1 * m3
m5.value
21
```

There are many more special methods, including methods for bitwise operations and for defining container-like objects that support slicing. For a full list of special methods, see https://docs.python.org/3/reference/datamodel.html#special-method-names.

Inheritance

One of the most important and powerful concepts in object-oriented programming is inheritance. With inheritance, a class declares another class or classes as a parent(s). The child can use the methods and variables from its parents as if they were declared in its definition. Listing 14.10 defines a class, Person, and then uses it as a parent class for another class, Student.

Listing 14.10 **Basic Inheritance**

```
class Person():
    def __init__(self, first_name, last_name):
        self.first_name = first_name
        self.last_name = last_name


class Student(Person):
    def introduce_yourself(self):
        print(f'Hello, my name is {self.first_name}')



barb = Student('Barb', 'Shilala')
barb.first_name
'Barb'

barb.introduce_yourself()
Hello, my name is Barb
```

Notice that the method Student.introduce_yourself() uses the variable Person.first_name as if it were declared as part of the Student class. If you check the type of the instance, you see that it is Student:

```
type(barb)
__main__.Student
```

Importantly, if you use the isinstance() function, you can see that the instance is both an instance of the Student class:

```
isinstance(barb, Student)
True
```

and an instance of the Person class:

```
isinstance(barb, Person)
True
```

Inheritance is useful when you are writing code that expects some shared behaviors across classes. For example, if you are implementing a job orchestration system, you might expect that every type of job has a run() method. Instead of testing for every possible job type, you can just define a parent class with a run() method. Any job that inherits from, and is therefore an instance of, the parent class will have the run() method defined, as shown in Listing 14.11.

Listing 14.11   **Testing for a Base Class**

```
class Job():
    def run(self):
        print("I'm running")

class ExtractJob(Job):
    def extract(self, data):
        print('Extracting')

class TransformJob(Job):
    def transform(self, data):
        print('Transforming')

job_1 = ExtractJob()
job_2 = TransformJob()
for job in [job_1, job_2]:
    if isinstance(job, Job):
        job.run()
I'm running
I'm running
```

If a child class defines a variable or method with the same name as is defined in its parent, instances of the child will use the child's definition. For example, say that you define a parent class with a run() method:

```
class Parent():
    def run(self):
        print('I am a parent running carefully')
```

Also say that you define a child class that redefines the method:

```
class Child(Parent):
    def run(self):
        print('I am a child running wild')
```

Instances of the child will then use the child class's definition:

```
chile = Child()
chile.run()
I am a child running wild
```

There are times when it is useful to call a parent class's method explicitly. For example, it is not unusual to call a parent class's __init__() method from within the child class's __init__() method. The super() function accesses the parent class and its attributes. The following example uses super() to call Person.__init__() from the child class Student:

```
class person():
    def __init__(self, first_name, last_name):
        self.first_name = first_name
        self.last_name = last_name


class student(person):
    def __init__(self, school_name, first_name, last_name):
        self.school_name = school_name
        super().__init__(first_name, last_name)

lydia = student('boxford', 'lydia', 'smith')
lydia.last_name
'smith'
```

Inheritance is not limited to one parent or one level. A class can inherit from a class, which itself inherits from another class:

```
class A():
    pass


class B(A):
    pass


class C(B):
    pass


c = C()
isinstance(c, B)
True


isinstance(c, A)
True
```

A class can also inherit from multiple parents:

```
class A():
    def a_method(self):
        print(A's method)
```

```
class B():
    def b_method(self):
        print(B's method)

class C(A, B):
    pass

c = C()
c.a_method()
A's method

c.b_method()
B's method
```

> **Note**
>
> In general, I advise against constructing overly complex inheritance trees when possible. Complex inheritance can become very difficult to debug as you trace the interactions between variables and methods defined through the tree.

> **Note**
>
> There has been much writing on object-oriented design. I recommend researching it further before embarking on a large object-oriented project to avoid unnecessary pitfalls.

Summary

Object-oriented programming involves grouping data and functionality in objects that are defined by classes. Special methods let you define classes that will work with Python's operators and classes, which implement container behavior. Classes can inherit definitions from other classes.

Questions

1. What does the variable self represent in a class definition?

2. When is the __init__() special method called?

3. Given the following class definition:

```
class Confuzed():
    def __init__(self, n):
        self.n = n
    def __add__(self, O):
        return self.n - O
```

what result would you expect from the following?

```
c = Confuzed(12)
c + 12
```

4. What will be the output of the following code?

```
class A():
    def say_hello(self):
        print('Hello from A')

    def say_goodbye(self):
        print('Goodbye from A')

class B(A):
    def say_goodbye(self):
        print('Goodbye from B')

b = B()
b.say_hello()
b.say_goodbye()
```

15

Other Topics

The most important property of a program is whether it
accomplishes the intention of its user.

C.A.R. Hoare

In This Chapter

- Sorting lists
- Reading and writing files
- `datetime` objects
- Regular expressions

This chapter covers some Python Standard Library components that are powerful tools for both data science and general Python use. It starts with various ways to sort data and then moves to reading and writing files using context managers. Next, this chapter looks at representing time with `datetime` objects. Finally, this chapter covers searching text using the powerful regular expression library. It is important to have at least a high-level understanding of these topics as they are all highly leveraged in production programming. This chapter should give you enough familiarity with these topics that you will understand them when you need them.

Sorting

Some Python data structures, such as lists, NumPy arrays and Pandas DataFrames, have built-in sorting capabilities. You can use these data structures out of the box or customize them with your own sorting functions.

Lists

For Python lists you can use the built-in `sort()` method, which sorts a list in place. For example, say that you define a list of strings representing whales:

```
whales = [ 'Blue', 'Killer', 'Sperm', 'Humpback', 'Beluga', 'Bowhead' ]
```

If you now use this list's `sort()` method as follows:

```
whales.sort()
```

you see that the list is now sorted alphabetically:

```
whales
['Beluga', 'Blue', 'Bowhead', 'Humpback', 'Killer', 'Sperm']
```

This method does not return a copy of the list. If you capture the return value, you see that it is None:

```
return_value = whales.sort()
print(return_value)
None
```

If you want to create a sorted copy of a list, you can use Python's built-in `sorted()` function, which returns a sorted list:

```
sorted(whales)
['Beluga', 'Blue', 'Bowhead', 'Humpback', 'Killer', 'Sperm']
```

You can use `sorted()` on any iterable, including lists, strings, sets, tuples, and dictionaries. Regardless of the iterable type, this function returns a sorted list. If you call it on a string, it returns a sorted list of the string's characters:

```
sorted("Moby Dick")
[' ', 'D', 'M', 'b', 'c', 'i', 'k', 'o', 'y']
```

Both the `list.sort()` method and the `sorted()` function take an optional `reverse` parameter, which defaults to `False`:

```
sorted(whales, reverse=True)
['Blue', 'Sperm', 'Beluga', 'Killer', 'Bowhead', 'Humpback']
```

Both `list.sort()` and `sorted()` also take an option `key` argument that is used to define how the sorting should be defined. To sort whales using the length of the strings, for example, you can define a lambda that returns the string length and pass it as the key:

```
sorted(whales, key=lambda x: len(x))
['Blue', 'Sperm', 'Beluga', 'Killer', 'Bowhead', 'Humpback']
```

You can also define more complex key functions. The following example shows how to define a function that returns the length of a string, unless that string is `'Beluga'`, in which case it returns 1. This means that as long as the other strings have a length greater than 1, the key function will sort the list by string length, except for `'Beluga'`, which is placed first:

```
def beluga_first(item):
    if item == 'Beluga':
        return 1
    return len(item)


sorted(whales, key=beluga_first)
['Beluga', 'Blue', 'Sperm', 'Killer', 'Bowhead', 'Humpback']
```

You can also use `sorted()` with classes that you define. Listing 15.1 defines the class Food and instantiates four instances of it. It then sorts the instances by using the attribute `rating` as a sort key.

Listing 15.1   **Sorting Objects Using a Lambda**

```
class Food():
    def __init__(self, rating, name):
        self.rating = rating
        self.name = name

    def __repr__(self):
        return f'Food({self.rating}, {self.name})'

foods = [Food(3, 'Bannana'),
         Food(9, 'Orange'),
         Food(2, 'Tomato'),
         Food(1, 'Olive')]

foods
[Food(3, Bannana), Food(9, Orange), Food(2, Tomato), Food(1, Olive)]

sorted(foods, key=lambda x: x.rating)
[Food(1, Olive), Food(2, Tomato), Food(3, Bannana), Food(9, Orange)]
```

If you call `sorted()` on a dictionary, it will return a sorted list of the dictionary's key names. As of Python 3.7 (see https://docs.python.org/3/whatsnew/3.7.html), dictionary keys appear in the order in which they were inserted into the dictionary. Listing 15.2 creates a dictionary of whale weights based on data from https://www.whalefacts.org/how-big-are-whales/. It prints the dictionary keys to demonstrate that they retain the order in which they were inserted. You then use `sorted()` to get a list of key names sorted alphanumerically and print out the whale names and weights, in order.

Listing 15.2   **Sorting Dictionary Keys**

```
weights = {'Blue': 300000,
           'Killer': 12000,
           'Sperm': 100000,
           'Humpback': 78000,
           'Beluga':  3500,
           'Bowhead': 200000 }

for key in weights:
    print(key)
Blue
Killer
Sperm
Humpback
Beluga
Bowhead
```

```
sorted(weights)
['Beluga', 'Blue', 'Bowhead', 'Humpback', 'Killer', 'Sperm']

for key in sorted(weights):
    print(f'{key} {weights[key]}')
Beluga 3500
Blue 300000
Bowhead 200000
Humpback 78000
Killer 12000
Sperm 100000
```

Pandas DataFrames have a sorting method, .sort_values(), which takes a list of column names that can be sorted (see Listing 15.3).

Listing 15.3 **Sorting Pandas DataFrames**

```
import pandas as pd
data = {'first': ['Dan', 'Barb', Bob'],
        'last': ['Huerando', 'Pousin', 'Smith'],
        'score': [0, 143, 99]}

df = pd.DataFrame(data)
df


       first    last        score
0      Dan      Huerando      0
1      Bob      Pousin       143
2      Bob      Smith         99

df.sort_values(by=['last','first'])


       first    last        score
0      Bob      Pousin       143
1      Bob      Smith         99
2      Dan      Huerando      0
```

Reading and Writing Files

You have already seen that Pandas can read various files directly into a DataFrame. At times, you will want to read and write file data without using Pandas. Python has a built-in function, open(), that, given a path, will return an open file object. The following example shows how I open a configuration file from my home directory (although you can use any file path the same way):

```
read_me = open('/Users/kbehrman/.vimrc')
read_me
<_io.TextIOWrapper name='/Users/kbehrman/.vimrc' mode='r' encoding='UTF-8'>
```

You can read a single line from a file object by using the `.readline()` method:

```
read_me.readline()
'set nocompatible\n'
```

The file object keeps track of your place in the file. With each subsequent call to `.readline()`, the next line is returned as a string:

```
read_me.readline()
'filetype off\n'
```

It is important to close your connection to a file when you are done, or it may interfere with the ability to open the file again. You do this with the `close()` function:

```
read_me.close()
```

Context Managers

Using a context manager compound statement is a way to automatically close files. This type of statement starts with the keyword `with` and closes the file when it exits its local state. The following example opens a file by using a context manager and reads it by using the `readlines()` method:

```
with open('/Users/kbehrman/.vimrc') as open_file:
    data = open_file.readlines()
```

```
data[0]
'set nocompatible\n'
```

The file contents are read as a list of strings and assigned to the variable named data, and then the context is exited, and the file object is automatically closed.

When opening a file, the file object is ready to read as text by default. You can specify other states, such as read binary (`'rb'`), write (`'w'`), and write binary (`'wb'`). The following example uses the `'w'` argument to write a new file:

```
text = 'My intriguing story'
```

```
with open('/Users/kbehrman/my_new_file.txt', 'w') as open_file:
    open_file.write(text)
```

Here's how you can check to make sure the file is indeed created:

```
!ls /Users/kbehrman
Applications    Downloads      Movies       Public
Desktop         Google Drive   Music        my_new_file.txt
Documents       Library        Pictures     sample.json
```

JSON is a common format for transmitting and storing data. The Python Standard Library includes a module for translating to and from JSON. This module can translate between JSON strings and Python types. This example shows how to open and read a JSON file:

```
import json
```

```
with open('/Users/kbehrman/sample.json') as open_file:
    data = json.load(open_file)
```

datetime Objects

Data that models values over time, called *time series data*, is commonly used in solving data science problems. In order to use this kind of data, you need a way to represent time. One common way is to use strings. If you need more functionality, such as the ability to easily add and subtract or easily pull out values for year, month, and day, you need something more sophisticated. The Datetime library offers various ways to model time along with useful functionality for time value manipulation. The datetime.datetime() class represents a moment in time down to the microsecond. Listing 15.4 demonstrates how to create a datetime object and access some of its values.

Listing 15.4   **datetime Attributes**

```
from datetime import datetime

dt = datetime(2022, 10, 1, 13, 59, 33, 10000)
dt
datetime.datetime(2022, 10, 1, 13, 59, 33, 10000)

dt.year
2022

dt.month
10

dt.day
1

dt.hour
13

dt.minute
59

dt.second
33

dt.microsecond
10000
```

You can get an object for the current time by using the datetime.now() function:

```
datetime.now()
datetime.datetime(2021, 3, 7, 13, 25, 22, 984991)
```

You can translate strings to datetime objects and datetime objects to strings by using the datetime.strptime() and datetime.strftime() functions. Both of these functions rely on format codes that define how the string should be processed. These format codes are defined in the Python documentation, at https://docs.python.org/3/library/datetime.html#strftime-strptime-behavior.

Listing 15.5 uses the format codes %Y for a four-digit year, %m for a two-digit month, and %d for a two-digit day to create a datetime from a string. You can then use the %y, which represents a two-digit year, to create a new string version.

Listing 15.5   **datetime Objects to and from Strings**

```
dt = datetime.strptime('1968-06-20', '%Y-%m-%d')
dt
datetime.datetime(1968, 6, 20, 0, 0)

dt.strftime('%m/%d/%y')
'06/20/68'
```

You can use the datetime.timedelta class to create a new datetime relative to an existing one:

```
from datetime import timedelta
delta = timedelta(days=3)

dt - delta
datetime.datetime(1968, 6, 17, 0, 0)
```

Python 3.9 introduced a new package, called zoneinfo, for setting time zones. With this package, it is easy to set the time zone of a datetime:

```
from zoneinfo import ZoneInfo

dt = datetime(2032, 10, 14, 23, tzinfo=ZoneInfo("America/Jujuy"))
dt.tzname()
'-03'
```

> **Note**
>
> As of the writing of this book, Colab is still running Python 3.7, so you may not have access to zoneinfo yet.

The datetime library also includes a datetime.date class:

```
from datetime import date

date.today()
datetime.date(2021, 3, 7)
```

This class is similar to datetime.datetime except that it tracks only the date and not the time of day.

Regular Expressions

The last package covered in this chapter is the regex library, re. Regular expressions (regex) provide a sophisticated language for searching within text. You can define a search pattern as a string and then use it to search target text. At the simplest level, the search pattern can be exactly the text you want to match. The following example defines text containing ship captains and their email addresses. It then searches this text using the `re.match()` function, which returns a match object:

```
captains = '''Ahab: ahab@pequod.com
              Peleg: peleg@pequod.com
              Ishmael: ishmael@pequod.com
              Herman: herman@acushnet.io
              Pollard: pollard@essex.me'''
```

```
import re
re.match("Ahab:", captains )
<re.Match object; span=(0, 5), match='Ahab:'>
```

You can use the result of this match with an `if` statement, whose code block will execute only if the text is matched.

```
if re.match("Ahab:", captains ):
    print("We found Ahab")
We found Ahab
```

The `re.match()` function matches from the beginning of the string. If you try to match a substring later in the source string, it will not match:

```
if re.match("Peleg", captains):
    print("We found Peleg")
else:
    print("No Peleg found!")
No Peleg found!
```

If you want to match any substring contained within text, you use the `re.search()` function:

```
re.search("Peleg", captains)
<re.Match object; span=(22, 27), match='Peleg'>
```

Character Sets

Character sets provide syntax for defining more generalized matches. The syntax for character sets is some group of characters enclosed in square brackets. To search for the first occurrence of either 0 or 1, you could use this character set:

```
"[01]"
```

To search for the first occurrence of a vowel followed by a punctuation mark, you could use this character set:

```
"[aeiou][!,?.;]"
```

You can indicate a range of characters in a character set by using a hyphen. For any digit, you would use the syntax `[0-9]`, for any capital letter, `[A-Z]`, or for any lowercase letter, `[a-z]`. You can follow a character set with a `+` to match one or more instances. You can follow a character set with a number in curly brackets to match that exact number of occurrences in a row. Listing 15.5 demonstrates the use of character sets.

Listing 15.6   **Character Sets**

```
re.search("[A-Z][a-z]", captains)
<re.Match object; span=(0, 2), match='Ah'>

re.search("[A-Za-z]+", captains)
<re.Match object; span=(0, 4), match='Ahab'>

re.search("[A-Za-z]{7}", captains)
<re.Match object; span=(46, 53), match='Ishmael'>

re.search("[a-z]+\@[a-z]+\.[a-z]+", captains)
<re.Match object; span=(6, 21), match='ahab@pequod.com'>
```

Character Classes

Character classes are predefined groups of characters supplied for easier matching. You can see the whole list of character classes in the `re` documentation (see https://docs.python.org/3/library/re.html). Some commonly used character classes are `\d` for digital characters, `\s` for white space characters, and `\w` for word characters. Word characters generally match any characters that are commonly used in words as well as numeric digits and underscores.

To search for the first occurrence of a digit surrounded by word characters, you could use `"\w\d\w"`:

```
re.search("\w\d\w", "His panic over Y2K was overwhelming.")
<re.Match object; span=(15, 18), match='Y2K'>
```

You can use the + or curly brackets to indicate multiple consecutive occurrences of a character class in the same way you do with character sets:

```
re.search("\w+\@\w+\.\w+", captains)
<re.Match object; span=(6, 21), match='ahab@pequod.com'>
```

Groups

If you enclose parts of a regular expression pattern in parentheses, they become a group. You can access groups on a match object by using the `group()` method. Groups are numbered, with group 0 being the whole match:

```
m = re.search("(\w+)\@(\w+)\.(\w+)", captains)

print(f'Group  0 is {m.group(0)}')
Group  0 is ahab@pequod.com
```

```
print(f'Group  1 is {m.group(1)}')
Group  1 is ahab
```

```
print(f'Group  2 is {m.group(2)}')
Group  2 is pequod
```

```
print(f'Group  3 is {m.group(3)}')
Group  3 is com
```

Named Groups

It is often useful to refer to groups by names rather than by using numbers. The syntax for defining a named group is as follows:

```
(?P<GROUP_NAME>PATTERN)
```

You can then get groups by using the group names instead of their numbers:

```
m = re.search("(?P<name>\w+)\@(?P<SLD>\w+)\.(?P<TLD>\w+)", captains)
```

```
print(f'''
Email address: {m.group()}
Name:  {m.group("name")}
Secondary level domain: {m.group("SLD")}
Top level Domain: {m.group("TLD")}''')
Email address: ahab@pequod.com
Name:  ahab
Secondary level domain: pequod
Top level Domain: com
```

Find All

Until now, you have only been able to find the first occurrence of a match. You can use the `re.findall()` function to match all occurrences. This function returns each match as a string:

```
re.findall("\w+\@\w+\.\w+", captains)
['ahab@pequod.com',
 'peleg@pequod.com',
 'ishmael@pequod.com',
 'herman@acushnet.io',
 'pollard@essex.me']
```

If you have defined groups, `re.findall()` returns each match as a tuple of strings, with each string beginning the match for a group:

```
re.findall("(?P<name>\w+)\@(?P<SLD>\w+)\.(?P<TLD>\w+)", captains)
[('ahab', 'pequod', 'com'),
 ('peleg', 'pequod', 'com'),
 ('ishmael', 'pequod', 'com'),
 ('herman', 'acushnet', 'io'),
 ('pollard', 'essex', 'me')]
```

Find Iterator

If you are searching for all matches in a large text, you can use re.finditer(). This function returns an iterator, which returns each subsequent match with each iteration:

```
iterator = re.finditer("\w+\@\w+\.\w+", captains)
```

```
print(f"An {type(iterator)} object is returned by finditer" )
An <class 'callable_iterator'> object is returned by finditer
```

```
m = next(iterator)
f"""The first match, {m.group()} is processed
without processing the rest of the text"""
'The first match, ahab@pequod.com is processed
without processing the rest of the text'
```

Substitution

You can use regular expressions for substitution as well as for matching. The re.sub() function takes a match pattern, a replacement string, and a source text:

```
re.sub("\d", "#", "Your secret pin is 12345")
    'Your secret pin is #####'
```

Substitution Using Named Groups

You can refer to named groups in a replacement string by using this syntax:

```
\g<GROUP_NAME>
```

To reverse the email addresses in the captains text, you could use substitution as follows:

```
new_text = re.sub("(?P<name>\w+)\@(?P<SLD>\w+)\.(?P<TLD>\w+)",
                  "\g<TLD>.\g<SLD>.\g<name>", captains)
```

```
print(new_text)
Ahab: com.pequod.ahab
Peleg: com.pequod.peleg
Ishmael: com.pequod.ishmael
Herman: io.acushnet.herman
Pollard: me.essex.pollard
```

Compiling Regular Expressions

There is some cost to compiling a regular expression pattern. If you are using the same regular expression many times, it is more efficient to compile it once. You do so by using the re.compile() function, which returns a compiled regular expression object based on a match pattern:

```
regex = re.compile("\w+: (?P<name>\w+)\@(?P<SLD>\w+)\.(?P<TLD>\w+)")
regex
re.compile(r'\w+: (?P<name>\w+)\@(?P<SLD>\w+)\.(?P<TLD>\w+)', re.UNICODE)
```

This object has methods that map to many of the re functions, such as match(), search(), findall(), finditer(), and sub(), as demonstrated in Listing 15.7.

Listing 15.7 **Compiled Regular Expression**

```
regex.match(captains)
<re.Match object; span=(0, 21), match='Ahab: ahab@pequod.com'>

regex.search(captains)
<re.Match object; span=(0, 21), match='Ahab: ahab@pequod.com'>

regex.findall(captains)
[('ahab', 'pequod', 'com'),
 ('peleg', 'pequod', 'com'),
 ('ishmael', 'pequod', 'com'),
 ('herman', 'acushnet', 'io'),
 ('pollard', 'essex', 'me')]

new_text = regex.sub("Ahoy \g<name>!", captains)
print(new_text)
Ahoy ahab!
Ahoy peleg!
Ahoy ishmael!
Ahoy herman!
Ahoy pollard!
```

Summary

This chapter introduces data sorting, file objects, the Datetime library, and the re library. Having at least a passing knowledge of these topics is important for any Python developer. You can do sorting either with the sorted() function or object sort() methods, such as the one attached to list objects. You can open files by using the open() function, and while files are open, you can read from them or write to them. The Datetime library models time and is particularly useful when dealing with time series data. Finally, you can use the re library to define complicated text searches.

Questions

1. What is the final value of sorted_names in the following example?

   ```
   names = ['Rolly', 'Polly', 'Molly']
   sorted_names = names.sort()
   ```

2. How would you sort the list nums = [0, 4, 3, 2, 5] in descending order?

3. What cleanup specific to file objects does a context manager handle?

4. How would you create a datetime object from the following variables:

```
year = 2022
month = 10
day = 14
hour = 12
minute = 59
second = 11
microsecond = 100
```

5. What does \d represent in a regular expression pattern?

A

Answers to
End-of-Chapter Questions

The answers to the questions at the end of each chapter are listed here.

Chapter 1

1. Jupyter notebooks.

2. Text and code.

3. Use the Mount Drive button in the Files section of the left navigation.

4. Python in Google Colab.

Chapter 2

1. `int`

2. They will execute as normal.

3. `raise LastParamError`

4. `print("Hello")`

5. `2**3`

Chapter 3

1. `'a' in my_list`

2. `my_string.count('b')`

3. `my_list.append('a')`

4. Yes

5. `range(3, 14)`

Chapter 4

1. `dict(name='Smuah', height=62)`

   Or

   `{'name':'Smuah', 'height':62}`

   Or

   `dict([['name','Smuah'],['height',62]])`

2. `student['gpa'] = 4.0`

3. `data.get('settings')`

4. A mutable object has data that can be changed; an immutable object has data that cannot be changed after its creation.

5. `set("lost and lost again")`

Chapter 5

1. `Biya []`

2. Hiya Henry

3.
```
for x in range(9):
     if x not in (3, 5, 7):
          print(x)
```

Chapter 6

1. `'after-nighttime'`

2. `'before-nighttime'`

3. An error.

4. `@standard_logging`

5. a
    b
    1

Chapter 7

1. NumPy arrays contain only one data type.

    NumPy arrays do element by element operations.

    NumPy arrays have matrix math methods.

2. `array([[1, 3],`

    `[2, 9]])`

3. `array([[0, 1, 0],`

    `[4, 2, 9]])`

4. `5, 2, 3`

5. `poly1d((6,2,5,1,-10))`

Chapter 8

1. `stats.norm(loc=15)`

2. `nrm.rvs(25)`

3. `scipy.special`

4. `std()`

Chapter 9

1. `df = pd.DataFrame({'Sample Size(mg)':[ 0.24, 2.34, 0.0234 ],`

    `'%P':                    [40, 34, 12 ],`

    `'%Q':                    [60, 66, 88 ]})`

    Or

    `df = pd.DataFrame([[ 0.24, 40, 60 ],`

    `[ 2.34, 34, 66],`

    `[0.0234, 12, 88 ]],`

    `columns=[ 'Sample Size(mg) ', '%P', '%Q' ])`

2. `df['Total Q'] = df['%Q']/df['Sample Size(mg)']`

   Or

   `df['Total Q'] = df.loc[:,'%Q']/df.loc[:,'Sample Size(mg)']`

   Or

   `df['Total Q'] = df.iloc[:,2]/df.iloc[:,0]`

3. `df.loc[:, ['%P', '%Q']] / 100`

Chapter 10

1. `plt.plot(data['X'], data['Y']`

2. `plt.plot(data['X'], data['Y'])`

3. ```
   fig, (ax1, ax2) = plt.subplots(1, 2)
   ax1.plot(data['X'], data['Y'])
   ax2.plot(data['X'], data['Y1'])
   fig.show()
   ```

   Or

   ```
   fig, (ax1, ax2) = plt.subplots(1, 2)
   ax1.plot('X','Y', data=data)
   ax2.plot('X','Y1', data=data)
   fig.show()
   ```

Chapter 11

1. Transform data.

2. To avoid overfitting.

3. Test the model's accuracy.

Chapter 12

1. ```
   gutenberg.words('austen-emma.txt')
   gutenberg.sents('austen-emma.txt')
   gutenberg.paras('austen-emma.txt')
   ```

2.
```
alice = gutenberg.words('carroll-alice.txt')
alice['Alice']
```

3.
```
alice = gutenberg.words('carroll-alice.txt')
alice_r = []
for word in alice_w:
    if word not in string.punctuation:
        if word.lower() not in english_stopwords:
            alice_r.append(word)
alice_dist = nltk.FreqDist(alice_r)
alice_dist.tabulate(10)
```

4.
```
alice = Text(gutenberg.words('carroll-alice.txt'))
alice.similar('rabbit')
```

5.
```
nltk.download('names')
names = nltk.corpus.names
all_names = names.words('male.txt')
all_names.extend( names.words('female.txt') )
hamlet_w = gutenberg.words('shakespeare-hamlet.txt')
hamlet_names = []
for word in hamlet_w:
    if word in all_names:
        hamlet_names.append(word)

hamlet_dist = nltk.FreqDist(hamlet_names)
hamlet_dist.most_common(5)
```

Chapter 13

1. 4
   4

2.
```
list(map(lambda x: f'{x}'*2, 'omni'))
```

Or

```
list(map(lambda x: f'{x}{x}', 'omni'))
```

3.
```
sum([x for x in range(100, 2)])
```

4.
```
(x**2 for x in range(1000))
```

5.
```
def fib():
    f0 = 0
    f1 = 1
    while True:
        yield f0
        f0, f1 = f1, f0 + f1
```

Chapter 14

1. The current instance of the class.

2. When an object is instantiated.

3. 0

4. `Hello from A`
    `Goodbye from B`

Chapter 15

1. `None`

2. `nums.sort(reverse=True)`

3. Closing the file object.

4. `datetime(year, month, day, hour, minute, second, microsecond)`

5. A digit.

Index

S

Register Your Product at informit.com/register

Access additional benefits and **save 35%** on your next purchase

- Automatically receive a coupon for 35% off your next purchase, valid for 30 days. Look for your code in your InformIT cart or the Manage Codes section of your account page.

- Download available product updates.

- Access bonus material if available.*

- Check the box to hear from us and receive exclusive offers on new editions and related products.

Registration benefits vary by product. Benefits will be listed on your account page under Registered Products.

InformIT.com—The Trusted Technology Learning Source

InformIT is the online home of information technology brands at Pearson, the world's foremost education company. At InformIT.com, you can:

- Shop our books, eBooks, software, and video training
- Take advantage of our special offers and promotions (informit.com/promotions)
- Sign up for special offers and content newsletter (informit.com/newsletters)
- Access thousands of free chapters and video lessons

Connect with InformIT—Visit informit.com/community

Addison-Wesley • Adobe Press • Cisco Press • Microsoft Press • Pearson IT Certification • Que • Sams • Peachpit Press

 Pearson